To Pastor *illegible*

We serve a
mighty God !

Blessings
to You.

Richard Ahee

A Light in the Darkness

By

Richard D. Lee

The story of four men called by God to
help survivors in Banda Aceh, Indonesia
following the devastating tsunami of 2004

ISBN 0-7414-2705-2

Back cover photo by Chuck Needy

Edited by
Victoria Giraud   Allan Manuel
Sherman Oaks, CA   Silver Spring, MD

Published by:
INFI∞ITY
PUBLISHING.COM
1094 New DeHaven Street, Suite 100
West Conshohocken, PA 19428-2713
Info@buybooksontheweb.com
www.buybooksontheweb.com
Toll-free (877) BUY BOOK
Local Phone (610) 941-9999
Fax (610) 941-9959

Printed in the United States of America
Printed on Recycled Paper
Published August 2005

Religion that God, our Father, accepts as pure and faultless is this: **to look after orphans and widows in their distress** *and to keep oneself from being polluted by the world.* *(James 1:27)*

Dedication

This book is dedicated to Hak Seng Soh—his friends call him Samuel—an unsung hero and one of the first Christians to arrive in the Muslim province of Aceh in response to the tragic tsunami devastation, and to the other men, women, and children who have donated their time, talent, and resources to help the survivors recover from this tragedy of biblical proportions.

Foreword

Although this story takes place in tsunami-ravaged Indonesia, it is not so much about the tsunami, as it is about God's intricate plan for our lives, and how one small part of God's unique plan for my life was interwoven with a portion of His special plan for the lives of others.

God has declared that before He formed us in our mothers' wombs, He knew us. And before we came forth from the womb, He had determined our destiny and designed a plan for our lives. (Jeremiah 1:5)

Samuel Soh and I had been unrepentant sinners for most of our lives, but God had preordained our meeting as Christians in Banda Aceh, a Muslim stronghold in the world's most populous Muslim nation—a place where Islamic *Shari`ah* or sacred Muslim law takes precedence over Indonesian law. In fact, proselytizing by other religions is forbidden. The ultimate penalty—death—is meted out to those caught violating this prohibition.

Since 1976, separatist Muslim rebels in the Aceh province have sought independence from the central government in Jakarta, the capital of the archipelago. Their desire for self-government has evolved into an armed conflict with Indonesian armed forces.

Introduction of the *Shari`ah* and the on-going conflict between the rebels and the military have made it difficult for outsiders, especially Christians, to visit the Aceh province.

While I don't believe that God caused the tsunami, I do believe that when the Indonesian government temporarily suspended its travel restrictions to the Aceh province, it was God opening the doors to this region for Christians to demonstrate Christ's love through their love, giving, and work. The tsunami also caused the Muslim people of Banda Aceh and the surrounding communities to cry out to God for help. No matter what our religious beliefs or spiritual condition, we sincerely seek God to intercede when we come face-to-face with death or suffer tragic loss and pain.

God did not turn His back on the cries of the Muslim people; He sent thousands of Christians, including Samuel Soh and our small team of four men, into the devastated areas as a visible manifestation of His love, comfort, and support. I don't pretend to know God's plan for the people we helped in the Internal Displaced Persons Camp #85, I only know that He has one, and that by His grace, we were a small part of that plan.

Our small team faced many self-imposed difficulties preparing for our trip: increased stress levels associated with our fundraising efforts, discouragement when we couldn't find an American relief organization to sponsor us, and a few internal disagreements and self-doubts about whether God really wanted us to go.

God never said it would be easy, He just said, "Go!" We're glad we did because we learned that when God sets His plan in motion, He provides the wherewithal to accomplish it. (Romans 8:28)

Because our inexperience required us to depend more on Him and to pray constantly for His favor and guidance, it brought us closer to God.

They say that hindsight is 20/20—I see now that God was in total control of our trip and perfectly managed every detail.

Chapter One

The Indian Ocean Earthquake-Tsunami

Mon Ikeun, Indonesia
26 December 2004

The early morning sun had brightened a pale blue, cloudless sky over the small beach community of Mon Ikeun, a small fishing village in the Muslim province of Aceh, on the northwestern coast of Sumatra in Indonesia. David Lines, a trim clean-shaven 40-year-old Australian, his Indonesian wife, Nurma, and their 3-year-old son were up early preparing for a day at the beach. It was Sunday, December 26, 2004. Their day was starting out as any other in paradise.

The fantastic waves in Aceh had drawn David, an avid surfer, to the area. After marrying Nurma, a local woman, six years ago, he built his dream house, constructed of concrete and cinderblock with a tiled roof, near the beach. The Lines lived six months of the year in Mon Ikeun and the other six months in Australia, where David is a partner/owner of The Marquee Venue, a hip-hop nightclub in Sydney. By all measures, he considered himself blessed with a good life!

Mon Ikeun and the other communities of Lam Kruet, Lam Lhom, Lambaro, Lampuuk and Lampayah are located

1

on or near the beautiful beaches of Lhok Nga, a middle-class district and recreational area of more than 20,000 residents just twenty kilometers (almost thirteen miles) southwest of the provincial capital of Banda Aceh.

These communities enjoyed the area's only golf course and tennis and volleyball courts. The white sandy beaches and clear blue waters of Lhok Nga made it the perfect spot for surfing, swimming, snorkeling, fishing, and boating. Every Sunday, the beaches were filled with the citizens of Lhok Nga and the residents of Banda Aceh. They would spend the afternoon and evening on the beach eating barbecue fish and drinking coffee and tea.

Being near the equator, weather in the area was normally in the mid-eighties, sometimes in the nineties. The rainy season, when heavy storms usually occur in the afternoon or at night, is between November and April. As a result of the tropical climate, local vegetation is dense and quite lush. Here, one can find a wide variety of tropical trees and plants.

Before the beaches were filled with people that Sunday, local residents felt a severe rumbling that lasted almost five minutes. This devastating earthquake, with a magnitude of 9.0 on the Richter scale, struck at 7:58 a.m. Immediately, many houses and buildings were damaged or collapsed, roadways buckled and trees fell throughout the Lhok Nga district.

David reacted instantly, calling to his wife to grab their son, a few belongings, and to get into the car. Before he joined his family, however, he had to get a quick glimpse of the ocean. From an open space near his home, about ten minutes after the quake, he could see the water receding, revealing a normally submerged coral reef. Moments later, he heard three loud booms from the ocean and saw a large wave forming. He knew instinctively they were in imminent danger from the water, but he didn't know how devastating it would be. "It looked like a big green barrel and not a bad looking wave," he said, but he wasn't going to wait around to see.

David raced back to the house and jumped in the car, where his wife and son were anxiously waiting. After having to drive toward the wave, they turned and headed northeast on the main road to Banda Aceh. On the way, he picked up people walking along the road and yelled warnings to others to get to higher ground as soon as possible. As he briefly looked back at the beach, he could see a wave rushing through the trees.

As he drove inland he could see the quickly rising Raba Lhok Nga River overflowing onto the road; ahead, the road was congested with cars, trucks, motorbikes, and pedestrians fleeing the area, and in some places the road was blocked by debris from collapsed buildings.

Within minutes, David was stuck in traffic. He quickly decided to take a detour toward a volleyball court at the base of a nearby hill. "I wanted to save the car; I knew this was big, but I didn't know how big." After parking his car and making sure all his passengers were out, he shouted to others fleeing the disaster to follow him as he and his family headed for the top of the hill.

The first giant fifty-foot wave came ashore just as David and almost a hundred people reached the safety of the summit. "Just as we got to the top of the hill, we were surrounded by raging water," David remembered. "There were multiple waves, up to ten, and then another series of two. The waters were rising, trees below were falling down and debris was getting really thick and moving fast. It was like a logging camp gone mad."

Roiling black water surged across the entire landscape right up to the mountains in the distance. Standing on their hilltop sanctuary, feeling the ground shake from continuous aftershocks, the survivors watched the raging water violently rush at them from all sides. Men, women, and children cried and prayed aloud to Allah.

The waves crushed almost everything that remained below as the water pushed through the once peaceful valley toward the city of Banda Aceh. Later, the debris-filled water made a slow withdrawal to the ocean.

"After an hour the water slowed down to a crawl and we began to notice people. I'm jumping in the water with an inner tube and saving them. The problem with saving people at that stage wasn't the water, because I'm a surfer. The problem was getting through the debris, which was hundreds of meters wide: wood with nails in it, corrugated iron, refrigerators, dead animals, but no dead bodies at that stage," David explained.

David's family and the others who'd escaped remained on the hilltop for the rest of the day and night. By the next morning the water had receded, and they could all see for the first time the totality of destruction that the tsunami had caused. The communities of Lhok Nga had disappeared along with most of the inhabitants and all of the homes.

Although he said he didn't see any dead bodies during the tsunami, David added, "I've seen about 500 bodies since then. My wife's family lost thirty of its members. Eighty percent of my village is dead and one hundred percent of the homes are wiped out...gone!"

Chapter Two

Joel's Bungalows

Lampuuk, Indonesia
26 December 2004

In the village of Lampuuk (population 6,500), just three kilometers (1.8 miles) north of Mon Ikeun, the staff of Joel's Bungalows was up early making preparations for the large crowds who gathered each Sunday on the soft sandy beaches.

Starting with a single bungalow in 1998, it had taken Zuifitri, "Joel", a 33-year-old Indonesian, five years to accomplish his lifelong dream of building beach bungalows for visitors to the beautiful beaches of Lampuuk. Now there were twelve, each with its own *mandi* (a local word for bathroom), and Joel had even added a large restaurant.

The bungalows were an immediate success with the locals and the foreign workers from the various humanitarian organizations serving the area. They had also become a favorite gathering place for the world's most experienced surfers who came to challenge Aceh's giant waves during the surfing season that ran from November to April. No matter who you were or where you came from, Joel, his Italian-born wife, Patrizia, and the staff of Joel's Bungalows treated every guest like a Hollywood star and welcomed them all with a spirited, "Welcome to paradise!"

Joel's Bungalows also provided employment and business opportunities for many of the residents of Lampuuk and the surrounding communities. The local fishermen sold their daily catch to the restaurant. Women of the village sold fresh cakes and donuts, vegetable curry, pineapple jam, and other local delicacies to the restaurant. Other businesses in the village benefited, too, especially the *labi labi* (the local taxis) used for transportation between the bungalows and Banda Aceh or the airport. Joel also provided financing for many small businesses in Lampuuk and helped people start small gardens for chili, watermelon, and rice.

The success of Joel's Bungalows was drastically impacted in May 2003, when peace talks between the Indonesian government and separatist rebels broke off, causing the government to impose a temporary six-month period of martial law in the Aceh province. One month later, a presidential decree severely restricted travel to the Aceh province, forcing foreigners out and prohibiting humanitarian organizations from working there.

Joel sent Patrizia to Italy to wait for the lifting of martial law. They didn't anticipate an extension of martial law for an additional six months, or the replacement of martial law with civil emergency restrictions in May 2004. Both actions delayed Patrizia's return to Indonesia. While in Italy, Patrizia started the process for Joel to obtain Italian residency. Joel departed for Italy on December 14, 2004, to complete the process.

Anticipating a short stay in Italy, Joel had left his capable staff, Aki, Andi, and Edi to handle things during his absence. On this fateful Sunday, they were in the office early making sure that the bungalows and the restaurant would be ready for the business on what was sure to be a busy day.

Shopkeepers throughout the village were doing the same. Sunday was their only opportunity to make up for the loss of business caused by the imposition of the martial law and civil emergency decrees. They'd sell large amounts of coffee, tea, clove cigarettes, sodas, fried noodles, vegetable curry, steamed rice, barbecue fish, coconuts, pineapples, and fruit shakes. Visitors would also browse the batik shops and purchase music CDs and videos from the CD shop.

At sunset on Sundays, everyone would sit on the beach and watch the color of the sky change from blue to red. Thousands of bats would take to the sky from a nearby mountain cave, appearing as black smoke against the red sky. To everyone's delight, after sunset, Aki, Andi, and Edi would light a bonfire on the beach in front of the bungalows.

This Sunday started out differently. A powerful earthquake shook the village at 7:58 a.m., causing the frightened residents of Lampuuk to rush into the streets. They were relieved to see that the quake had only caused minor damage to their homes. A few shops had collapsed, several palm trees on the beach had fallen, and a few cracks appeared on the main roadway. Others near the beach noticed the sea receding, something they had never experienced before. Minutes later, several booms were heard from the sea when the beachgoers noticed a giant wall of water heading toward the shore. The people panicked and began running away from the beach in terror, yelling to others, "Run!...Run! Water is coming."

By 8:46 a.m., the entire village of Lampuuk and more than 6,000 residents had been washed away by a giant nintety-foot wave. The only semblance of civilization that remained of Lampuuk was the Rahmatullah Mosque.

In Italy, Joel and Patrizia watched in horror as the news broadcast showed the devastation caused by the tsunami. They learned several days later that Joel's mother and all of his relatives living in Lampuuk had been killed.[1]

---

[1] Those interested in contacting Joel and Patrizia or making donations for the restoration of Joel's Bungalows may contact them at patriziamasetti@yahoo.com.

Chapter Three

Hak Seng Soh

Today, at age thirty-four, his name is Samuel Soh, but his Chinese birth name is Hak Seng Soh. Samuel was born into a Buddhist family in Langsa, Indonesia, a small town on the northeastern coast of the Aceh province on the island of Sumatra.

He grew up in a nearby province, in the city of Medan. After finishing high school, Samuel enrolled in Reinhardt College in Waleska, Georgia, intending to major in engineering. In his sophomore year, Samuel transferred to DeKalb College, now Perimeter College in Atlanta. He transferred again at the beginning of his senior year to Southern Polytechnic State University in Marietta, where he studied industrial engineering.

To pay for his education, Samuel worked in a restaurant and pizzeria. Prior to completing his senior year, Samuel left school to work full time, a decision he still regrets, although his desire for learning continues to burn strong.

Samuel studied on his own to become a computer technician and received a diploma from CompTia, which gave him highly respected credentials in the computer technology field. Before long he'd completed the curriculum offered by Microsoft and became a Microsoft Certified Systems Engineer. Not stopping there, Samuel eventually became a Cisco Certified Networking Professional. With these credentials, Samuel became a self-employed computer network contractor.

In 1994, Samuel began studying philosophy, reading books by philosophers Bertrand Russell, Thomas Paine and Voltaire. Their logical reasoning eventually convinced him there was no God, and in due course he gave up the Buddhist traditions he had cherished since childhood and became an atheist.

During the 1996 Summer Olympic Games in Atlanta, he met a beautiful Indonesian Christian woman named Pita Tarigan. The first day she met him, when he admitted he was an atheist, she told Samuel he needed to be saved. "You can try," he replied.

Their relationship was touch-and-go for a while, but she eventually accepted him for what he was. They became engaged at the end of 1997. He occasionally attended Pita's church and watched with skepticism as people were delivered from evil spirits and instantly healed from many medical problems. Later he attended a Christian crusade with Pita; because he suffered from frequent migraines, she insisted that he go to the altar for a healing. He was reluctant at first, but when he went to the front he was healed immediately. "I started to question my atheism and wanted to believe that the healing was God's work."

What truly brought Samuel to Christ was the supernatural experience he had approximately one week later. He woke up abruptly one morning at 4 a.m. and felt an unknown presence in his bedroom. He and the room were filled with overwhelming feelings of rage and hate. All the things in the room, including the furniture, started to talk to him loudly. At first he logically thought he was hallucinating, but as the experience continued, he began to lose control and he talked back, having a fierce conversation with a bedroom lamp as he walked backward and forward.

He felt on the brink of insanity and sensed the presence of a deep crevasse into which he could fall, and from which there would be no return. Like a super-imposed film, childhood memories flashed before his eyes. He saw himself as a child kneeling down and praying. For the very first time in his life, he fell to his knees and called on the name of Jesus, then he confessed his sins and repented. Suddenly the entire room returned to normal, with no noise other than his own breathing and his rapid heartbeat. He felt a deep sense of peace, which seemed familiar, yet ancient. When he told Pita about his experience, she told him it had been a spiritual battle and that Jesus had won.

On the day of their wedding in 2000, Pita whispered to Samuel that she would take him home to Indonesia, now that he was a Christian. Over the next couple of years she became increasingly homesick for her own country and insisted they return to Indonesia. But because Samuel saw Indonesia as a country full of corruption, hate, and sin, a place unfit for raising their newborn daughter, Erin, he resisted.

One day near the end of 2003, God spoke to Samuel's heart, showing him how he'd spent a lot of time in the past chasing the wrong investments in life. God told Samuel He had a plan for his life; it was time to serve and live for Him and return to Indonesia. He and his wife sold all their assets and in January 2004, they moved to the Indonesian City of Medan, where they became very active in a local church.

On Monday, December 27, 2004, Samuel had been watching television news when they broadcast the tragedy of the tsunami destruction along the northwestern coast of Aceh, the province of his birth. "I've got to go to Banda Aceh to help," he told Pita immediately.

At first, Pita resisted his leaving, but she eventually saw it was God sending him home to minister to the people. "Go, follow your heart. God shall be with you," Pita declared as she hugged Samuel and let him go.

Samuel made his way to a nearby military airbase and attempted to register as a volunteer, but he was rejected outright because he didn't have a sponsoring organization. He contacted his pastor and received a letter appointing him as a church volunteer. He returned to the airport but had to wait two days before being allowed to depart for Banda Aceh on an Australian military plane.

Samuel arrived in Banda Aceh on the morning of December 30. He started helping right away by loading survivors onto the plane he'd flown in on, which was returning to Medan.

As he made his way into Banda Aceh, the cloud-covered sky made the empty city look eerie. Rotting corpses were everywhere, the air reeked of death, and aftershocks continued to shake the ground, but Samuel was not afraid. God had given him peace of mind.

There were very few people in the city because the survivors had fled to the airport or to the nearby hills. In the city, Samuel joined up with an Indonesian Search and Rescue (SAR) team that had just arrived from Jakarta.

They headed for Lhok Nga to the west of Banda Aceh, and searched for survivors. They found two survivors that evening and immediately transported them to the military hospital, where Samuel saw seriously injured patients lying side-by-side on the floor waiting for care.

Many patients died that day because there weren't enough doctors to handle the number of injured people crowded into the small emergency unit. Patients waiting to be seen shared the same room with dead bodies piled into one corner.

The SAR team, being prudent and cautious of rebel activity, returned to their temporary camp at the airport after working all day. Samuel, who was a civilian without proper credentials, could not accompany them to their camp. Instead, he remained alone in the dark city at night, sleeping among the thousands of corpses and tons of debris that blanketed the streets.

Every morning the SAR team would come back and pick him up to continue their search for survivors. Because of the delay in getting out of Medan, Samuel was already out of the small amount of food he had brought with him, and had very little water left. Not wanting to become a burden to the SAR team, he decided to fast and did so for three days. He chose to look at his situation positively: not eating meant he didn't worry about getting to a bathroom.

During the first week, many of the survivors found in the debris were excited to see their rescuers. Some would grab hold and cling so tightly it seemed they'd never let go. Others, in a deep state of depression or distraught because of lost loved ones, and the loss of all their possessions, didn't want to be rescued—they just wanted to be left alone to die. Apart from those that managed to escape, the SAR team picked up everyone they came across.

The second week Samuel and the SAR team began to sweep the hills, going deeper into the woods in search of survivors who might be too traumatized to come down for help. During one search, Samuel was alone when he encountered several Muslim rebels. When he explained what he was doing, they told him not to worry, he was not their target. He surmised they were probably on the lookout for Indonesian military personnel.

After leaving the SAR team, Samuel worked with *Medan Peduli* (Medan Care), now called *Bersama Membangun Aceh* (Together We Build Aceh), where he helped distribute food and organize logistics. At the request of his pastor, a few days later he joined World Harvest, a large Christian Indonesian humanitarian and community development organization. With World Harvest, he helped to provide medicine, health care, and counseling to the survivors in Internal Displaced Persons Camp #85 (IDP Camp #85).

Chapter Four

The World Takes Notice

On Sunday, December 26, 2004, my family and I were preparing to head back home to Maryland from a visit to Ohio. My wife, Annette (nicknamed Peppe) and I, my youngest son, Jonathan, my wife's sister, Peni, and our niece, Teresa, had been visiting family in Bedford Heights, Ohio, a small community near Cleveland at the intersection of I-271 and I-480. Normally a six-hour drive, I knew it would take longer this time because the snow-covered roads would be clogged with other homeward-bound travelers who were expected at work on Monday morning. My Ford Excursion had four-wheel drive and handled the road well in these conditions, but the additional traffic and white-out conditions would demand caution, and that meant taking it slow and easy.

My middle son, Alex, who lives in Ohio, and his friend, Deon, an Episcopal priest, were joining us for the return trip home. After waiting for Father Deon to complete his Sunday morning and afternoon obligations, we finally got on the road at 6:30 p.m.—a late start for me because I dread driving at night, especially on the mountainous highways of western Pennsylvania and Maryland.

We passed the hours listening and singing along to several CDs of hits from the '60s and '70s. As it turned out, traffic wasn't as heavy as expected and the roads were relatively clear, even though it had continued to snow until we reached Maryland. The trip took only two additional hours to complete. When we finally arrived home around 2:00 a.m., everyone was exhausted and immediately went to bed.

* * * * *

According to my wife, I'm a news hog because at home I keep the television on one of the cable news channels. If I'm in my car, the radio is usually tuned to the local all-news station. I really can't help it: my father was a journalist and I once owned a weekly community newspaper, so, you might say, news is in my blood. Despite my being a news hog, I had totally missed the news of the Indian Ocean earthquake and tsunami as we prepared to leave Ohio to return to Maryland.

Most Americans, like me, were focused on getting home and enjoying a week of leisure after the Christmas holiday and in advance of the upcoming New Year's celebrations. During the first few days after the tragedy, the news hardly stirred public reaction because we Americans are a visually stimulated people, and there were few early videos of the disaster.

I had caught up on the latest tsunami-related news by midweek as numerous videos from Sri Lanka and Thailand began dominating news broadcasts. At that time, casualty numbers were still uncertain. The early videos from North Sumatra and the high casualty estimates there, which seemed to increase hourly, caught everyone by surprise.

America and other nations began sending military assistance teams to provide immediate help. Dignitaries from various countries were dispatched to assess the damage, including Colin Powell; America's outgoing Secretary of State, and Jeb Bush, the Governor of Florida and President George Bush's younger brother. It had taken almost a week, but the nations of the world were finally mobilizing to provide whatever assistance was necessary for the affected region.

Chapter Five

The Tsunami Phenomenon

I spent most of New Year's weekend researching tsunamis. I vaguely recalled hearing about tsunamis in the past, but I couldn't remember ever hearing about one that had caused casualties.

A tsunami (pronounced soo-nah-mee), I learned, is Japanese for "*harbor wave.*" It is generally believed that the term was created by Japanese fishermen who returned to port to find the area surrounding their harbor devastated, although they had not encountered any wave in the open water.

A series of underwater waves, generated by a spontaneous disturbance that vertically displaces the water, causes a tsunami. These waves can travel great distances at tremendous speeds and wreak havoc on coastlines as they come ashore. They are caused by underwater earthquakes, landslides, volcanic eruptions, explosions, and even the impact of extraterrestrial bodies, such as meteorites.

Contrary to public belief, most tsunamis do not produce giant breaking waves, but rather, come ashore as very strong, swiftly moving tides resulting from a rapid rise in sea level. Much of the damage is caused by strong currents and floating debris that travel much farther inland than normal waves.

I was amazed when I learned of a 9.5 magnitude earthquake that occurred on May 22, 1960, off the coast of Chile, triggering a Pacific-wide tsunami. It was the largest recorded earthquake of the twentieth century. Approximately 2,300 people perished as a result: 2,000 along the Chilean coast, sixty-one in Hawaii where the tsunami struck almost fourteen hours after the quake; 138 in Japan; and thirty-two dead and missing in the Philippines.

Another giant earthquake occurred in 1964 off the coast of Alaska. The resulting Pacific-wide tsunami from that 9.3 magnitude quake killed more than 120 people in Alaska, Hawaii, British Columbia, Washington, Oregon, and California.

I was even more astonished to learn that tsunamis occur quite frequently. Information available from the International Tsunami Information Center in Honolulu, Hawaii, reports thirteen killer tsunamis since 1990. (I created a *Table of Killer Tsunamis Since 1990* that appears at the end of this chapter).

The frequency and potential of deadly tsunamis in the Pacific Ocean caused the United Nations Educational, Scientific and Cultural Organization (UNESCO) and the United States to build two tsunami early warning centers. Hosted by the United States, one center is located in Alaska to serve as the regional Tsunami Warning Center for Alaska, British Columbia, Washington, Oregon, and California. The other is located in Hawaii to serve as the regional Tsunami Warning Center for Hawaii, but it also coordinates tsunami warnings for twenty-six Pacific Rim nations. These centers monitor earthquakes. If the location and magnitude of an earthquake meets the criteria for generating a tsunami, a warning is issued of the impending danger.

Unfortunately, there are no tsunami early warning systems covering the Indian Ocean region, the Atlantic Ocean basin or the Mediterranean. Two groups, however, are working to establish tsunami early warning programs in the Caribbean. UNESCO has proposed the establishment of an Intra-Americas Sea Tsunami Warning System and the United

States Federal Emergency Management Agency has sponsored the development of a Puerto Rico Tsunami Warning and Mitigation Program. Both programs are still in the developmental stages.

The tragedy of December 26, which unfolded on television screens around the world, is now forcing many governments to seriously consider establishing a global tsunami early warning system.

Richard D. Lee

Table of Killer Tsunamis Since 1990

Location	Date of Occurrence	Lives Lost
Nicaragua	September 2, 1992	170
Okushiri Island, Japan	July 12, 1993	239
Flores Island, Indonesia	December 12, 1992	1,690
East Java, Indonesia	June 2, 1994	222
Kuril Island, Russia	October 4, 1994	11
Mandoro, Philippines	November 15, 1994	78
Manzanillo, Mexico	October 9, 1995	1
Irian Jaya, Indonesia	February 17, 1996	110
Ocona, Peru	February 21, 1996	12
Papua, New Guinea	July 17, 1998	2,182
Vanuatu, S.W. Pacific	November 26, 1999	5
Sulawesi Island, Indonesia	May 3, 2000	46[*]
Ocona, Peru	June 23, 2001	96

* Indicates the combined death toll from the earthquake and tsunami.

Chapter Six

God Implements His Plan

On Wednesday morning, January 5, 2005, the Fox News Channel aired a tsunami video that I had not seen before. The video actually showed the tsunami striking a city in northern Indonesia. I watched as advancing water enveloped what appeared to be a marketplace. People ran for cover into the nearby shops. In the next frames, the video showed the streets and shops inundated with water and floating debris (David Lines so aptly described it as a "logging camp gone mad"). There were floating cars, trees, refrigerators, lumber, parts of houses, and people caught up in the fast moving black water as it rushed through the streets, leaving nothing in its wake.

I watched in horror as one scene showed an old woman wearing a head scarf sitting in the back of a blue pickup truck. Next to her was a teenage boy, most likely her grandson. The truck and its passengers were caught up in the steadily rising water, being carried along with the other debris. The teenager was desperately looking for a way to escape, but the old woman was sitting calmly, resigned to her impending fate. I knew from having watched the videos from Sri Lanka and Thailand that they would not survive. At that moment I felt a longing in my spirit to go there—I couldn't explain it then, but I knew for sure I was needed there. And at that point I wasn't even sure where *there* was.

I changed the channel to CNN in time to watch the video again. This time I caught the name of the city. It was called Banda Aceh. A quick internet Google search revealed that it was the capital of Aceh, the northernmost province on the island of Sumatra in Indonesia. A population of more than 4.2 million lived within approximately 60,000 square kilometers (23,160 square miles)—about the size of the State of West Virginia.

I sat in silence for a long time trying to reason with myself and understand the urging in my spirit that was pushing me forward. It seemed like a crazy idea. *Why would God call a 57-year-old disabled veteran with no building experience to go to a place that needed rebuilding?* It didn't make sense. I'd spent the last twenty years as a public servant handling matters of public policy at the senior-levels of the United States government. My expertise was in writing, organizing, and management. Did I forget to add that my financial situation was already stretched to the limit? Simply put, it seemed like an impossible task.

In the last two years, however, I'd ventured out of my comfort zone and volunteered for several construction-related mission trips with my church, the Evangel Assembly of God, Camp Springs, Maryland. On those trips, I worked as a "gofer," merely there to support the other experienced workmen. I did little things like carry blocks, mix cement, cut short lengths of steel rebar (construction reinforcing bars), or just made sure the other workmen had whatever they needed. I didn't think for a minute that any of those experiences qualified me to go to Banda Aceh, but, still, I was convinced God was calling me to go there.

My first action was to call the Assistant Pastor of my church, Pastor Eric Dorsey, who, like me, is a former Marine. He manages the church's missions ministry, which has recently undertaken trips to Mexico, Dominica, Nicaragua, and West Virginia.

At age forty-five, he is still trim and fit in a solid six-foot frame. He operates a very successful home improvement business. If he agreed to go, his vast building expertise would be invaluable on the ground in Indonesia.

He was supportive of the project. He and I agreed that we would have to form a very small group for this project. He would also seek the approval of the Senior Pastor and call me back.

I was on pins and needles for the rest of the day while I waited for him to get back to me. I left work around 4:30 p.m. and headed home without hearing back from him. I knew I'd get a chance to talk with him later that evening at our Wednesday night church service.

I honestly don't remember much about that service because my mind was still focused on going to Indonesia. As the service came to a close, the Senior Pastor announced that the church would be sending four men to Indonesia. That grabbed my full attention.

After the service, I walked quickly over to Assistant Pastor Dorsey and thanked him for getting the Senior Pastor's approval for the project, and scolded him in a playful way for not calling me back with the good news. With the Senior Pastor's approval in hand, we now needed to raise the money to cover some of our expenses for the trip.

Without thought or hesitation and with a confidence that surely wasn't mine, I told him we could raise the money. The moment was a little surreal; I was standing there, listening to my own self-assured words, but in my mind I was thinking, "That's it; it's over because I detest fundraising." I was no good at it, and would rather use my own money, even when my funds were low, than ask others for theirs. I realize now that it wasn't me speaking—the response had come from a higher source.

As we continued to discuss the trip, we were joined by a mutual friend, Richard Bell, an able-bodied fifty-two-year-old master plumber. Richard had served in the Army during the Vietnam War. He had accompanied me on mission trips to West Virginia and Nicaragua, and had joined

Pastor Eric on a mission trip to Los Angeles. In addition to his plumbing expertise, he also possessed some degree of knowledge of the electrical and carpentry trades. On our trips to Matagalpa, Nicaragua, and Newhall, West Virginia, I had witnessed his sincere love for God as we ministered to the local people. I also learned during those trips that he was a person you could count on when things got rough. He was on my short list for the trip.

I quickly told him about the trip and persuaded him to come along. He seemed a little reluctant at first, wanting to know what we would do there. Then he quickly added, "Aren't there bodies still lying in the streets? I don't think I can work with the bodies." I reassured him that the bodies had already been recovered, and that we would find work with one of the relief agencies distributing food or working to clear the debris.

"We'll have to raise our own money," I told him.

Like me, he had little or no experience with fundraising. "I'll give it try," he agreed.

"We can do it," I declared confidently. "Don't worry about it. Just say you're going to go."

"You can count on me!" he replied enthusiastically.

I then asked Pastor Eric about a fourth member, and he suggested taking someone along who knew the local language. The person he had in mind was Roy Ramalingam, a forty-two-year-old fitness center manager. Roy was a naturalized American citizen of Indian heritage who was born in Malaysia and spoke a Malay dialect called Bahasa Malaysia, which, as it turned out, is similar to Bahasa Indonesia. A Malaysian-speaking Bahasa Malaysia in Indonesia would be understood just as an Indonesian speaking Bahasa Indonesia would be understood in Malaysia. Born into a Hindu family, Roy had converted to Christianity at age seventeen and joined Youth With A Mission (YWAM)—one of the world's largest Christian youth mission organizations. He traveled with YWAM for four years throughout Asia and North America. He married an American member of YWAM in 1986 and became an American citizen in 2001.

Roy was a good choice. He had accompanied me and Richard on the mission trip to Nicaragua where we witnessed that he was a hard worker, a fast learner, and able to work independently.

Chapter Seven

The Favor of God

I was overjoyed on the drive home from the Wednesday night service—we were going to Banda Aceh! Of course, there was still the *small* matter of the fundraising, but I was happy to let God handle that. I had no real worries, or so I thought.

That night I received a warning in a dream. In my dream it was late afternoon. My cat, Charlie, a large Blue Russian, was standing at my front door, which was opened just enough to let him stick his head out. When I walked to the door to close it, Charlie took off for the kitchen. A powerful gust of wind pushed against the door. No matter how hard I pushed back, the door wouldn't close. Suddenly, the door burst open and an invisible force lifted me off my feet. I could feel the pressure, like a giant hand wrapped around my body, as I was being lifted up toward the ceiling above the staircase. I began repeating, "In Jesus name, in Jesus name," over and over, but the invisible force held me in place. Somehow, I knew that my wife, Peppe, was in our upstairs bedroom, but when I looked in that direction, I saw that the bedroom door was closed. I yelled "Peppe" at the top of my voice between repeated cries of "In Jesus name." My yelling finally awoke my wife, who shook me out of the nightmare.

The next morning, during our commute to work, my wife and I talked briefly about the nightmare. I told her I believed the dream was a warning from God that we would be under constant attack for undertaking the mission to Indonesia. Looking back, I'm convinced I was right because the dream caused me to pray continuously for God's favor and His presence on our journey. I'm delighted to say He was faithful in every way.

* * * * *

The first logistical step we needed to take was to arrange for travel. I researched the airlines flying into Indonesia. The lowest roundtrip fare I could find was a hefty $1,500, and that was separate from the additional $2,000 for our hotel and food expenses. Fortunately, the church would cover the expenses of the mission's team leader, so we'd only have to raise funds for three people. That meant we'd have to raise approximately $6,000.

During the week, I called several major humanitarian organizations to ask about working with them in Indonesia, but my calls were unfruitful. Beginning to feel a little discouraged, I decided to pray. I asked God for His favor in finding an organization for us to assist. I felt moved to try and contact an organization already working in Indonesia. I did a Google search for churches in Indonesia, but the only thing that came up was a website for International English Services (IES), which I thought was a translation business. This group came up no matter what search terms I used. Later in the day I opened the website and was surprised to see it was a Jakarta church conducting tsunami relief operations and that it was associated with my church's denomination.

Established in 1999, IES is an evangelistic church serving the entire English-speaking community of Jakarta, both expatriates and Indonesians, and is a part of the worldwide fellowship of Assemblies of God churches with over 35 million members all over the world. The IES website indicated it was providing relief to the Aceh province through Operation Blessing—a joint venture with other churches in Indonesia.

I composed the following e-mail and addressed it to Dave Kenney, who the website identified as the Pastor:

From: *Richard Lee*
Sent: *Thursday, January 6, 2005 3:10 p*
Subject: *Urgent Tsunami Assistance*
Importance: *High*

Blessings Brothers -

I'm sending this e-mail because we want to assist you on the ground with a small disaster relief team. We have already made monetary contributions to charitable organizations for the victims of the tsunami.

We will be dispatching our fast-response mission's group of four men, with seasoned skills in logistics, building, first aid, administration/organization, etc., to Jakarta on January 31 to assist with the humanitarian efforts. We would like them to join your efforts and they would do whatever your leadership instructs them to do. The men are former Marines and served in that part of the world during their careers. They would be self-sustained and fully supported by our church and available January 31 for 10 days.

I look forward to your reply. Our prayers are with you.

I received a simple reply the next morning:

From: *Dave and Gigi Kenney*
Sent: *Friday, January 07, 2005 6:10 p*
To: *Richard Lee*
Subject: *RE: Urgent Tsunami Assistance*

Thanks. I will work with others here to plan to make sure we can deploy your men where they can be most effective for Aceh and the Kingdom.

God had answered my prayers. I forwarded a copy to Pastor Eric and left an excited message about the response from IES on his cell phone.

* * * * *

I'd also researched visa requirements for Indonesia. According to the website of the Indonesian Embassy in Washington, D.C., we'd need to apply for visit visas—a process that normally takes up to ten days. In addition to completing a written application, the process required photos, copies of our roundtrip tickets, and a letter from our employer indicating our employment status.

I realized that we'd have to get moving on the visas right away and to do that we'd need airline tickets. I made a note to discuss it with the group.

Chapter Eight

The Resourcefulness of God

On the following day, Saturday, I worked on a fundraising flyer. I also called my brother and sister and asked for a donation. Both agreed.

I arrived at church early on Sunday to get Pastor Eric's approval for the fundraising flyer. I'd also brought along an empty five-gallon water bottle with a sign taped to the outside: *Tsunami Relief Fund.* I'd seeded the bottle with about twenty dollars in change, but I needed his permission to use the bottle to solicit spare change from members of the congregation.

I strolled into his office carrying the flyer and shaking the water bottle. "Did you see the e-mail from the church in Jakarta?" I asked enthusiastically, grinning like a Cheshire cat.

He hadn't had a chance to check his e-mails or listen to his voice messages because he'd gotten home late from a conference, so I told him briefly I'd found a sponsor in Indonesia. I showed him the flyer and asked him about using the bottle. He looked the flyer over and gave his approval but said he'd have to check with the Senior Pastor about using the bottle.

As I rushed out to the church's entrance hall to begin handing out the flyers, I stopped and asked the church clerk to make an announcement about donating to our trip. A few minutes later, Pastor Eric showed up with the bottle and said the Senior Pastor was okay with using it. I sat the bottle on a table in the entrance hall in full view of everyone entering or leaving the sanctuary.

When I told him later about the visa requirement for airline tickets, he said that once we raised half the money, the church would purchase the tickets. I was a little concerned that it would delay our trip because in reality we were a long way from the estimated $6,000 we needed.

I prayed silently that God would touch the hearts of people so they would give like they had in the Bible for the building of the temple—they had given so much the priests had to tell them to stop. (Exodus 36:5-6)

As I prayed, I remembered the Senior Pastor's words from months before, *"God's truth is greater than reality. God's truth can change reality."* Suddenly a church member approached the table and handed me a check for $500. Others came forth after the service and put their donations in the bottle. By late afternoon, we'd collected more than $1,300!

Contributions from our relatives, friends, neighbors, and co-workers started to pour in. And later, a special church offering raised more than $5,100. God didn't stop there, as contributions continued to flow in after we had departed for Indonesia.

With my hope renewed, I stepped out in faith and increased our goal to $10,000, and asked my sister-in-law to make a contribution chart on white poster board. She drew an oversized thermometer on the white board with tick-marks indicating each $100 of giving; she used a red magic marker to color in the total amount of contributions we'd received so far.

God showed us His resourcefulness as that goal was exceeded even before we departed.

Chapter Nine

The Blessings of God

On Monday morning, January 10, 2005, I went to the immunization clinic at Andrews Air Force Base to get several recommended inoculations and medicines. In addition to vaccines for hepatitis A and B, tetanus, influenza, and typhoid, travelers were advised to begin taking malaria pills, and to bring along an antibiotic effective for diarrhea and skin infections.

I was disappointed when told I needed a referral from my primary care physician; I knew that getting an appointment prior to our departure would be impossible. Since I'd already received vaccinations against tetanus and influenza, I decided to go without the other recommended precautions and hoped it wasn't a decision I would later regret.

Two days later I received an emergency call in my office from my wife's supervisor, who informed me that Peppe had temporarily lost sight in her left eye after experiencing a burst of intense white light. It was the same eye that had been operated on four years earlier to repair a detached retina.

The next morning I took her to the eye clinic at Walter Reed Army Medical Center. While we waited, I decided to go down the hall to the walk-in medical clinic. I was seen within minutes and the attending physician, Dr. Craig Bush, not only provided me with prescriptions for malaria pills and an antibiotic, but referred me immediately to the immunization clinic. There I received the other recommended vaccinations and returned to the eye clinic just as my wife returned from the examination room. Her news was equally good. Not finding anything wrong, the doctors told her she had probably experienced an ocular migraine—a vascular spasm affecting the blood supply to the vision center of the brain—usually caused by stress. They also told her the eye, especially the repaired retina, was in good shape.

On the drive home, we discussed the entire episode and realized that God had used a small burst of light to get me to Walter Reed so I would not depart for Indonesia without taking the necessary precautions. I learned later that one member of our team was unable to get malaria pills. I had more than enough and shared my pills with him.

What a wonderful God we serve!

* * * * *

At the beginning of the next week, Pastor Eric began making inquiries with Christian relief groups about tsunami relief opportunities for our team in Indonesia. In most cases, he was told that they had teams on the ground in Indonesia assessing the situation but couldn't offer anything at present. He did, however, learn of a travel agency that offered reasonable roundtrip fares to Indonesia.

Later in the afternoon, he contacted the travel agency and asked it to price our trip. Using an itinerary--Baltimore-Detroit-Tokyo-Singapore-Jakarta--the trip would take almost fifty hours to reach Jakarta, but the roundtrip price was only $1,186 dollars per person. Pastor Eric also learned we could get visas upon arrival at the airport in Jakarta, relieving us of the need to undergo the prolonged and tedious process at the Indonesia Embassy in Washington.

* * * * *

On Tuesday morning, January 11, I received an e-mail from a pastor in Indonesia asking if we could move up our departure date to January 21 to help set up a base camp for relief operations in Meulaboh, a remote city on Sumatra's west coast that had also been decimated by the tsunami.

> **From:** *Jeff Hartensveld*
> **Sent:** *Tuesday, January 11, 2005 10:16a*
> **To:** *Richard Lee*
> **Subject:** *Team*
>
> *Dear Richard,*
>
> *Dave Kenney in Jakarta has referred your name to me and forwarded your e-mail to me regarding your fast response team. I just returned from Aceh province after spending 5 days there assessing the situation. On or around the 24th of January we will be going to Meulaboh, in Aceh province, to set up a base camp to operate out of. (Something I have never done before). It seems that your men could assist us in this and advise us in the area of logistics if they are interested.*
>
> *And in possibly purchasing and bringing with them some good sturdy 8 men tents possibly army issue. Something that isn't that easy to come by here. Currently we are thinking of having them made here since we can't buy them ready made.*
>
> *It wouldn't be the actual ministry of delivering food and aid although some of that might happen but setting up our camp is of Primary Importance to the future of our ministry there as we are hoping to direct our aid to more long term assistance.*

I noticed in your e-mail that the team is talking about leaving on the 31st of January. By the 31st, and keeping in mind that if they leave on 31, they won't arrive here in Indonesia until the 2nd or 3rd of Feb., then getting to Aceh will take at least a day, we actually hope to be set up and have begun the process of operating by then. If there is someone else that needs the team it may be of more value at that time to go to another area.

I was excited that we were being offered a project but I wasn't really thrilled about changing our destination from Banda Aceh to Meulaboh because the vision God had given me was for Banda Aceh. After consulting with the group, I sent a response declining his proposal, but offered to purchase the tents. Pastor Jeff responded quickly:

From: *Jeff Hartensveld*
Sent: *Wed, January 12, 2005 8:40 a*
To: *Richard Lee*
Subject: *Re: Team*

Dear Richard,

The tents look great and actually I'm trying to get Convoy of Hope to FEDEX 3 of them to me tomorrow. Along with a different one that will be a command tent.

I got another e-mail from Dave saying you guys will hit the ground on 31st. I'm sorry but this won't work for us. Honestly, there are a lot of teams wanting to come. The only one I considered was yours because I think you could help us in the establishment of our camp. But the need that we have will be finished by the 31st.

And also the logistics of getting the team to Meulaboh on those days will be hard. From what I know, the only reasonable way to get supplies and people there is over land through rebel controlled territory. We are hoping to join a convoy leaving Medan on the 21st that will have an Indonesian military escort. I'm looking into helicopters flown by Heli Mission but the costs are usually huge and we will have to go through Banda Aceh and at this point I think I'm better off going over land because Banda is a nightmare for transportation.

Thanks again for your willingness to come but at this point I'm not sure it will work out. Maybe Dave can use you in another area.

I e-mailed Pastor Jeff and thanked him for considering us. We were back at square one.

* * * * *

For the rest of the week, we continued without success to contact various charitable and humanitarian organizations seeking volunteer opportunities in Indonesia.

On Sunday morning, January 23, 2005, the Senior Pastor called the team before the congregation. He prayed for each of us and, through the laying on of hands, bestowed a special anointing of the Holy Spirit on us for the work ahead. Later in the service, we were pleasantly surprised when he announced a special congregational offering for our trip. That offering raised over $5,100.

That evening another e-mail arrived from Pastor Jeff. His project had been delayed and he wanted to know if we were still interested.

While I felt encouraged by the e-mail, it still wasn't Banda Aceh. I sent off an e-mail to Pastor Dave Kenney at IES informing him that while we weren't turning down Pastor Jeff's new proposal, we really wanted something that would fit into our schedule—the thirty-first of January through the tenth of February.

I informed the other team members that Pastor Jeff's project in Meulaboh was back on the table but we'd have to wait to see if the government granted him permission to set up the base camp. I also told them I had e-mailed Pastor Dave and asked him to check with other organizations in Indonesia.

Later in the week Pastor Jeff e-mailed me with news that the government had granted permission for the base camp in Meulaboh. They needed our photos, passport numbers, and birth dates to complete the government process. We provided everything without delay and continued our departure preparations for the twenty-ninth of January.

* * * * *

Disappointing news arrived from Indonesia on Thursday evening, the twenty-seventh of January, two days before our departure. The base camp project was delayed again. That left us without a project and no prospects. I contacted Pastor Dave at IES one more time but he hadn't come up with anything. With less than forty-eight hours before our departure, things looked hopeless.

We'd raised the money to cover our expenses, purchased our airline tickets, and had scheduled the next day off from work to purchase items to take along and to pack our gear for the trip. *How could things go so wrong at the last minute?*

* * * * *

My wife stayed home from work with me on Friday. Over morning coffee, I told her about our lack of a project in Indonesia. Speaking firmly and confidently, she reminded me it was God's trip and He would work things out. "Just stay prepared," she said.

Later, we went out to pick up a few things from an army surplus store. We then stopped at one of the last remaining Little Tavern Hamburger stands for lunch. Not knowing what kind of food I'd be eating in Indonesia, I ate my all-American meal with relish.

After lunch I asked if she'd like to go to a movie and she accepted. We love the movies and because I'd be gone for two weeks, I thought it would be nice to treat her to one.

* * * * *

While we were sitting in the darkened theatre enjoying the movie and the popcorn, I couldn't help but think about our trip to Indonesia. We were departing in the morning without a project and needed an eleventh hour miracle. *Where was God?*

My thoughts were suddenly interrupted by the vibration of my cell phone indicating an incoming call. I was undecided about whether to answer or not, but at the last second I opened the cover. The caller ID screen revealed one word—*Unavailable*. I rose from my seat, stepped into the aisle, and answered the call.

They say God is never late, never early, but always right on time. I can certainly testify to that because the call was from God!

God used Lew Belcourt, an executive with World Harvest, a large Christian Indonesian humanitarian and community development organization. He was calling from Jakarta, Indonesia. "I thought you'd appreciate hearing directly from someone here in Indonesia," were his first words.

He told me he was a Lieutenant Colonel in the Marine Corps Reserve, and I knew immediately God was sending us a message because the Assistant Pastor and I are both former Marines. And the Marine Corps motto is *Semper Fidelis*, which is Latin for *"Always Faithful."* God was letting us know we could depend on Him because He truly is always faithful.

World Harvest was founded in 1989 by its current Chairman, Dr. Jimmy Oentoro. The Jakarta-based organization was helping people in a refugee camp in Banda Aceh, which housed more than 1,500 people in 250 tents. They needed someone to setup a large generator to provide electricity and lighting and to run pumps for water. Lew thought the project would require approximately six to seven days to complete. If we accepted the project, we'd have to purchase materials in Jakarta and transport them more than 1,200 miles by air to the camp.

I don't remember much more about the call except that we'd be working in Banda Aceh. My notes of the call are pretty skimpy:

Lew Belcourt
011-6221-547-xxxx
Lhok Nga
Wednesday morning
24,000
Tools
1500 residents

Although we had very little electrical experience, I accepted the project. Later that afternoon, I called the others to share the good news.

* * * * *

We departed from the Baltimore-Washington International Airport (BWI) at 9:30 a.m., on Saturday morning, January 29, 2005. In Detroit, we changed planes for the thirteen-hour flight to Tokyo. We had flown over the snowbound east coast of the United States, now we'd fly over parts of snow-covered Canada and Alaska.

We boarded a fully booked Boeing 747 for Tokyo and were seated in the rear coach section. Our flight attendants, Dave and Kelley (a husband and wife team), and another wonderful lady, whose name I don't remember but who contributed $20 to our mission, were fantastic. Cheerful and considerate, they treated us well and truly made the long, exhausting flight to Tokyo enjoyable. We were so excited about getting to Indonesia that all we could do was catnap.

After a two-hour layover and a plane change in Tokyo, we arrived in Singapore at midnight on January 31, 2005, facing a long, seven-hour layover before our final flight to Jakarta.

Roy Ramalingam's uncle and other members of his extended family who lived in Singapore were there to greet us. He asked them to take us into Singapore where we could get something to eat. He was especially interested in *Mee Goreng*, an ethnic Indian-Indonesian-Malaysian dish that he hadn't had since leaving Singapore almost eight years earlier. In Malay, *Mee Goreng* means "fried noodles," but he was interested in the Indian-style noodle dish, which contained a combination of onions, green peas, cabbage, bean sprouts, tomatoes, potatoes, eggs and Chinese greens. The ingredients are vigorously tossed in a wok with a spicy sauce.

His family took us to a late night food court, also called a "hawker center," because it's an outdoor market made up of twenty or more food stalls, serving a variety of food and drinks from Malaysia, India, China, and Indonesia. Each stall employs hawkers (one or more waiters) to aggressively compete for customers against hawkers from the other stalls.

While Roy enjoyed his *Mee Goreng*, the rest of us dined on four or five servings of delicious beef *satay* on bamboo skewers, otherwise known as barbecue on a stick. *Satay*, originally an Indonesian dish of long thin strips of chicken or beef threaded onto bamboo sticks, has caught on worldwide and now includes pork, seafood, and vegetables. The meat is marinated for several hours (and sometimes for days) in a variety of blended spicy and/or sweet ingredients, such as peanut sauce, that brings out the authentic Asian flavor.

The perils of eating outdoors were brought home to me when a stray calico-colored cat with a short tail with a kink at the end sauntered over to my backpack, which I had placed on the ground next to my chair. Much to my chagrin, he nonchalantly urinated all over my winter coat and my backpack. The others laughed while I went off to find some water to rinse off the articles before we returned to the airport.

After satisfying our appetites and being able to relax for a few hours, we were dropped off at the airport with plenty of time to check-in and board our final four-hour flight to Jakarta.

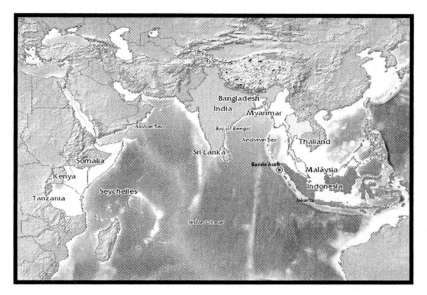

Photo 1 - Map of tsunami ravaged Indian Ocean countries.
(Courtesy of DM Solutions Group)

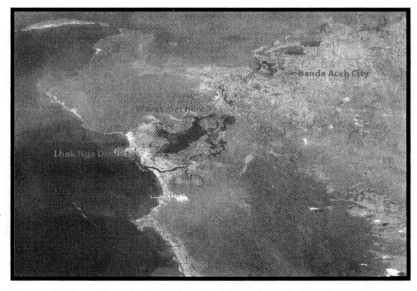

Photo 2 - Satellite photo of the Aceh Province in Northern
Sumatra, taken on December 29, 2004. (Satellite imagery courtesy of
Space Imaging)

Photo 3 - Satellite photo of the Lhok Nga District, taken on January 10, 2003, one year prior to the 2004 tsunami. (Satellite imagery courtesy of Space Imaging)

Photo 4 - Satellite photo taken of the Lhok Nga District on December 29, 2004, just three days after the 2004 tsunami. (Satellite imagery courtesy of Space Imaging)

Photo 5 - (February 2005) The hands on this clock mark the exact time that the two waves met in the valley between Banda Aceh and Lhok Nga. It now stands as a memorial to all who perished.

Photo 6 - (January 2005) A lone Mosque remains at Lampuuk.
(US Navy image courtesy of illinoisphoto.com)

Photo 7 - (January 2005) David Lines of Mon Ikeun in IDP Camp #85, Lhok Nga, Indonesia.

Photo 8 - (September 2002) Zuifitri "Joel" in the office of Joel's Bungalows. (Photo courtesy of Joel's wife, Patrizia Masetti)

Photo 9 - (January 2005) Hak Seng Soh - "Samuel" - the ground operations director for World Harvest in Banda Aceh, Sumatra, Indonesia. (Photo courtesy of World Harvest)

Photo 10 - (January 2005) Lew Belcourt , Vice President-Indonesia for World Harvest and his son, Scott, in Banda Aceh, Indonesia. (Photo courtesy of World Harvest)

Photo 11 - (February 2005) Team members pose at the entrance to IDP Camp #85, (l-r) Richard D. Lee, Roy Ramalingam, Pastor Eric Dorsey (Team Leader), and Richard Bell.

Photo 12 - (February 2005) Team members in the entrance to the Chief's tent after snacking on fried bananas and warm Jell-O.

Photo 13 - (February 2005) Many children are among the residents of IDP Camp #85. (Photo courtesy of World Harvest)

Photo 14 - (February 2005) Mixed emotions show on the faces of children in IDP Camp #85. (Photo courtesy of World Harvest)

Photo 15 - (February 2005) Humanitarian organizations, including World Harvest, engage the children in games. (Photo courtesy of World Harvest)

Photo 16 - (February 2005) Pastor Eric Dorsey (center) and the author (back right corner) with jubilant camp residents at an evening assembly celebrating the lighting of the camp.

Chapter Ten

Jakarta, Indonesia

When we finally touched down in Jakarta at 11:30 a.m. on January 31, we had been traveling a total of fifty exhausting hours. We felt like it, and to look at us, you'd agree. We had no trouble getting through immigration and customs with all bags intact. Despite our desire to get to a hotel and sleep in real beds, and despite the high humidity and temperature (probably in the 90s!), once we got our feet on the ground, we were reinvigorated by our mission and eager to get on with our work.

Our first order of business was to cancel our rental car. On our flight from Singapore, Robert, a native of Singapore, had cautioned us about the hazards of driving in Jakarta. For the past year, he'd worked in Jakarta during the week and returned home to Singapore to be with his family on the weekends.

In addition to our inexperience driving cars from the right side, and our inability to read street signs posted in Indonesian, he pointed out that Jakarta streets were hazardous and overcrowded with buses, trucks, cars, and motorbikes that followed no established rules of the road. He suggested we use taxis or hire a car with a driver.

We decided on the taxi. Because the taxis were small, we required two to carry the four of us and our bags to the hotel. On the way to the hotel, we saw firsthand Robert's forecast of crowded and perilous road conditions and were grateful he had been an angel sent from God!

Thousands of motorcyclists were weaving in and out of traffic, and drivers thought nothing of driving on the shoulder of the road. The noise was deafening. Smog control seemed unheard of, as countless old automobiles and buses belched smoke and stinking fuel oil into the air.

It was a long drive to the hotel and we had to pass through several tollbooths along the road; having no idea about currency exchange rates, we never would have made it in a rental car. Although we were halfway around the world, there were many familiar sights in this very cosmopolitan city: like skyscrapers, McDonalds, Burger King and Pizza Hut.

After arriving safely at our hotel, we had to go through several security checkpoints. We weren't surprised; before we left home, we had heard news about rebel activity in Indonesia and that relief workers might be targeted. With an active al Qaeda network in Indonesia, terrorists had already bombed the Marriott Hotel, the Australian Embassy and the Bali Nightclub. We later discovered that every hotel, department store, bank and apartment building in Jakarta had terrorist checkpoints, and that heightened our concern for our own safety.

The next surprise was the hotel itself. We only knew it was next door to International English Services. To our pleasant surprise, we discovered a Five Star Hotel with comfortable, plush rooms (two of us to a room) and large bathrooms boasting brass fixtures. After we'd put our luggage in our rooms, we took time to freshen up a bit and pray before heading next door to the International English Services Church to meet our host, Pastor Dave Kenney.

As we arrived, Pastor Dave and his staff were just finishing up a morning session of a conference on overcoming crisis situations. He greeted us warmly and invited us to have lunch with him.

Pastor Dave, a forty-eight-year-old American, is a large man, full of the Holy Ghost and the anointing of God. He was born in Washington State to missionary parents, who moved to Asia when he was just two years old. As a child, he lived in the Philippines and Malaysia, but came back to the States to attend Northwest College (now Northwest University) in Kirkland, Washington, from which he graduated in 1977. Following college he entered into fulltime ministry and lived in the Marshall Islands, Fiji, Hong Kong, Indonesia and the Philippines. He met his wife, Gigi, in 1985. In 1989 they were married, and now have a beautiful eight-year-old daughter named Isabel. In 1990, they moved to Indonesia and in 2000, they began working as pastors of the International English Services Church. As it turned out, Pastor Dave and Roy knew many of the same people in Malaysia.

After a Western lunch of deli sandwiches and soft drinks, Pastor Dave provided us with a short briefing on the history of the Aceh Province. He explained that the region is ruled by the Islamic *Shari`ah,* or sacred Muslim law, which prevents Christians from evangelizing the Muslim people of that area. Any violation could result in immediate death to the violator and would have a long-term negative impact on opportunities to evangelize the Acehnese people in the future.

"Your primary mission is to complete the work that World Harvest has assigned to you," he stated emphatically, then added, "Let your Christianity show through your work and through your love for the people."

His words were another confirmation that we were working under God's will. We had agreed before leaving home that our primary goal for coming to Indonesia was to help the survivors recover from the tragedy.

Pastor Dave repeated the information that Lew Belcourt had shared with me on our telephone call two days earlier, and he reminded us that we'd meet Lew the next day at the World Harvest Center headquarters.

At the end of the briefing, he gave us a list of materials Lew had suggested we purchase before departing for the camp. The list included one and a half miles of electrical cable, 250 lighting fixtures, a panel box with breakers, and 250 light bulbs. Pastor Dave had no information about the generator in the camp except to confirm we'd be working with 220-volt electrical current.

Pastor Dave provided us with an Indonesian electrician, and an Indonesian driver who could act as our interpreter. He then sent us into the local marketplace to purchase the electrical tools and materials we'd need to complete the work at the camp.

The local marketplace consisted of about ten electrical storefronts along one side of one block on a one-way street that had been closed off to traffic except for those purchasing goods from the local electrical merchants.

Here we were—four guys with very little electrical experience—making decisions to purchase materials to setup a mystery generator, which no one seemed to know anything about. To add to our predicament, our Indonesian driver-interpreter only spoke a few words of English and the materials offered for sale were of very poor quality.

Pastor Eric and Richard Bell, the only two in our small group with any electrical experience, took the lead in working with the local electrician to make the sales clerk understand what we wanted. I stood by, quietly praying for God's help. I was sure the others were doing the same.

They began making progress when they got the sales clerk to demonstrate the wiring connection between the panel box and the generator, which he accomplished without much difficulty. Then they asked the electrician to demonstrate the wiring of the lighting fixture, which he could not do since the only cable available was too large to fit into the hole in the top of the fixture.

Pastor Eric, with help from Richard, showed the electrician and the sales clerk how the connection would be made in the United States using a short run of two wires from the fixture to the main cable. Pastor Eric explained that electricians in America called it a "pigtail." When they had finished, both the electrician and the sales clerk studied the connection then smiled in agreement that the new connection was superior to what they had tried. Smiling broadly, they pronounced the new foreign word "pigtail" as they pointed approvingly at the connection.

Before leaving, we also purchased thirty rolls of electrical tape, two wire cutters, two hammers, four boxes of nails, six bags of wire nuts, and a special cable to connect the generator to the panel box.

Although we didn't have any information on the generator, both Pastor Eric and Richard seemed more confident about the wiring. On the way back to the hotel, Pastor Eric said he would call a master electrician who attends our church and seek his advice about wiring the generator and working with 220-volt current. Richard also suggested we begin making pigtail connections so that we'd have a head start when we reached the camp.

* * * * *

Early the next morning we met in Pastor Eric's room for our daily devotion. We talked about the faithfulness of God and how important it was for us to stay in prayer for God's continued favor and protection. It was another moment of confirmation for me because I'd been up since 3:00 a.m., drinking coffee while making diagrams of the camp where we would string up the lights among 250 tents, then praying and seeking God's favor and protection for the team. I also asked the Holy Spirit to give Pastor Eric and Richard the special knowledge and wisdom to handle whatever electrical challenges we would face. Although I knew that God had brought us to Indonesia and would take care of us, I still struggled with fear and felt responsible because I had convinced the others to come along.

After devotion, we headed down to the hotel's KAFE restaurant to enjoy its world-renowned breakfast buffet, a mixture of Western and Indonesian food, which was excellent. It was a wonderful treat, doubly so because it was included with the price of our rooms.

Later in the morning, we met briefly with Pastor Dave to thank him immensely for all of his help and hospitality, and to update him on our purchases. Our next move was to hire a taxi to take us to the headquarters of World Harvest.

The World Harvest Center is an impressive three-story building with a domed-roof auditorium that can hold 2,500 people. It was recently built on a manicured two-acre campus in the affluent suburb of Karawaci, about an hour's taxi ride from downtown Jakarta.

Founded in 1989, World Harvest works to improve the health and vitality of underserved communities through a variety of educational programs. It helps under-served communities by building proper sanitary facilities, providing medical care and serving nutritious food.

World Harvest also works with Fokus Pada Keluarga, an affiliate of Dr. James Dobson's twenty-five-year-old Focus on the Family, providing radio broadcasts of Bible-based family values to help people discover the true creator of families—Jesus Christ.

* * * * *

We arrived at the World Harvest Center just before noon on February 1, and instructed our driver to wait for us. Upon entering, we were ushered into an austere, windowless office where we met Lew Belcourt, a slender, forty-four-year-old American, who serves as Vice President-Indonesia for World Harvest.

It was an exciting moment for me as I stood face-to-face with the man, who, just several days earlier, had been the voice from God on the other end of the phone when I answered my cell phone in that darkened theatre back in Maryland.

After being seated, we were offered our choice of coffee, tea, or soft drinks. Lew sat down behind a large desk cluttered with piles of letters, newspapers, folders, and handwritten notes that were scattered over the entire desktop. In the very center, there was cleared a small work area.

After a short prayer, we took turns over the next hour, sharing our backgrounds and our Christian experience. Lew told us that he and his wife, Monica, had attended Old Dominion University in Norfolk, Virginia, where they had studied applied linguistics and received certifications for teaching English to speakers of other languages. Lew later earned a Master's of Divinity from Regent University in Virginia Beach, Virginia. Lew and Monica, accompanied by their two boys, Scott and Chris, then set off to Indonesia as missionaries.

I expected to meet a stiff-backed, ramrod straight, hard-charging, no-nonsense Marine Corps Officer, but Lew looked more like a scholarly college professor. He was balding and dressed casually in penny loafers, light brown khaki trousers, and a two-toned green polo shirt embroidered with the words "World Harvest" under the organization's logo.

His down-to-earth, easygoing style immediately set us at ease and provided some pretty hilarious moments for us. It also gave us an opportunity to get to know Lew as a proud husband and father, a scholar and an intellect, a man who had worked hard to achieve high rank in the Marine Corps, and a dedicated Christian missionary. Surprisingly, and to his credit, he was also a man who could laugh at himself.

One particular incident during the briefing caused us a great deal of amusement. In explaining the history and organizational structure of World Harvest, Lew stood up to draw a diagram on his whiteboard, which was covered with notes scribbled from a previous meeting. As he fumbled through the piles of clutter on his desk for an eraser, he spotted a crumpled napkin. It drew his attention and he was momentarily distracted as he carefully straightened the napkin and studied the writing scrawled on one side. Then with a shrug of his narrow shoulders, he turned and began using the napkin to erase the board.

"Those aren't important notes, are they?" Richard quipped, causing the rest of us to laugh.

"I don't know because I couldn't read my handwriting," Lew deadpanned without turning from the board.

We continued to laugh, but Lew remained straight-faced, focused on the task at hand.

After cleaning the whiteboard, he returned to his desk in search of a dry erase marker. Not finding one among the clutter, he excused himself and left the room.

He returned moments later holding a marker and announced, "I asked my Indonesian secretary for a dry erase marker. She gave me this one. I hope it's not a permanent marker."

"That looks like a permanent marker," Richard remarked.

"Well, I told her that I didn't want a permanent marker, but sometimes she finds my Indonesian difficult to understand. Let's hope she understood me this time." He made another cursory examination of the marker, which seemed to satisfy him, then began writing on the whiteboard. We laughed heartily later when he couldn't erase the permanent ink.

Lew was very gracious in allowing us a moment of hilarity at his expense, then continued the briefing with an overview of World Harvest operations in Banda Aceh and our work at the camp, which he estimated would take about six or seven days.

"What type of generator do they have in the camp?" Pastor Eric asked, still hoping for some specifics.

"Oh, I don't know, I've never visited the camp," Lew replied, "but my son, Scott, took some pictures while he was in the camp working as a translator for the group of doctors we'd sent up there." Lew pulled out a hidden computer mouse and began searching his hard drive for the photos. When he'd found them, he turned his monitor around for us to view. "The camp is pretty large," he continued as he scrolled slowly through the photos, "At last count there were 1,500 people living there in 250 tents. They've been without power and lights, and a working water pump for almost a month, so they'll be glad to see you."

Scott's photos were quite good and showed tents of various sizes and shapes, arranged haphazardly throughout the camp. When Lew reached the end of the photos, we sat back, a little disappointed there was still no photo of the mystery generator.

Near the end of the briefing, Lew told us that World Harvest had a three-bedroom house in Banda Aceh where we would reside during our stay. To our surprise, Lew also gave us a worldwide cell phone so we could stay in touch with him. The phone's security code was not in the box, so Lew stepped out to retrieve it from his secretary.

Roy took this opportunity to run out and tell our taxi driver we'd be a bit longer. Upon his return, he said the taxi driver was not pleased with our delay, so we'd better wrap it up. We were getting a little tired as our body clocks were still on Maryland time. I had jet lag almost the whole time we were in Indonesia, and I think the others did as well. Our body clocks never fully adjusted to the twelve-hour time difference.

Lew returned with the security code and four roundtrip tickets to Banda Aceh. He announced we were departing the next day on the first flight at 6:30 a.m., and would be met at the airport by Samuel Soh, an Indonesian believer in charge of ground operations for World Harvest in Banda Aceh.

Lew concluded the briefing on a precautionary note about penalties for evangelizing the Acehnese people, then led us downstairs to met Jacob, an Indonesian pastor with a million-dollar smile, who handled logistics for relief workers going to Banda Aceh.

Pastor Jacob gave each of us a heavy-duty backpack, two World Harvest shirts, a World Harvest baseball cap, and a one-day supply of bottled water and snacks. He also informed us we'd only be allowed to take whatever items we could fit into the backpack—which turned out to be just enough space to accommodate two changes of clothes and our toiletries. The army duffle bag I'd brought along, stuffed with candy and toys for the kids, would be an exception.

* * * * *

We arrived back at our hotel eager to pack for the trip to Banda Aceh. We stuffed as much as possible into the backpacks and left the rest in our suitcases, which we gave to the hotel concierge to hold in storage during our absence. In addition to two changes of clothes and my toiletries, I was able to pack a small first aid kit, a personal pack of pre-moistened toilet paper, two military ready-to-eat meals, six packs of instant oatmeal, and a week's supply of instant coffee. I intentionally left my Bible in my suitcase in Jakarta because I didn't want it to be the cause of a problem in Banda Aceh (a dumb act on my part because everyone else, including the Christian Indonesians at our base camp, had brought along their Bibles and used them every night during evening devotions).

Later in the evening, an IES staff member delivered an envelope to my room that contained five million rupiah—the currency of Indonesia—equivalent to about 500 U.S. dollars.

"What's this for?" I asked.

"You need it to pay excess baggage charges for the materials you're taking with you to Banda Aceh." Then he added, "We'll have someone bring all of your materials to the airport and they will assist you with getting them through the departure process."

Wow! IES and World Harvest were truly God sent. They had paid for all of the electrical supplies and materials, provided us with roundtrip plane tickets to Banda Aceh, gave us a place to stay once we arrived there, and now they were paying for the excess baggage. We felt like God was rolling out the red carpet for us. What a wonderful God we serve!

* * * * *

We were up and dressed by 3:00 a.m. and assembled in Pastor Eric's room for our morning devotion before heading for the airport. I was delighted to hear Pastor Eric and Richard announce for the first time they felt confident about completing the wiring job, as both had previously voiced concerns about the mystery generator. Because they were the only ones with any type of electrical experience, this was a relief for Roy and me. We ended our devotion with prayer for God's continued favor, presence, and protection.

We arrived at the airport two hours before our scheduled departure time, but couldn't check-in without our materials. An hour passed before our airport contact with the materials arrived. We learned that, unlike the rule in America, where passengers check-in at least two hours before the flight, Indonesia didn't seem to have such a requirement.

At the check-in counter, the airline representative informed us we would have to pay a substantial amount for our excess baggage. He suggested we send the materials by cargo plane and the airline would waive the costs because all relief materials going into the tsunami-ravaged area were carried free-of-charge on cargo flights.

It was a wonderful gesture, but we couldn't wait for the next cargo flight or take a chance our materials might get lost. In declining his generous offer, we explained we wanted to get the lights working in the camp as quickly as possible, so we'd need to take our materials on our flight. The counter clerk called his supervisor over and explained our mission, right on the spot. To our surprise and delight, the supervisor reduced the excess baggage charges by fifty percent. Then he assigned a military security guard to escort us and our materials to the secure baggage area where we personally gave our materials to the baggage handlers loading our flight.

Not once during the entire trip did anyone ask for a bribe in exchange for their assistance (like we'd heard about in other countries where relief supplies were delayed until money passed under the table). To the contrary, everyone readily offered their assistance to help us complete our mission. We were convinced that God was preparing the way for us and we praised Him continuously.

* * * * *

One thing had bothered me since arriving in Jakarta: It seemed to me that the Indonesian people in Jakarta were going about their normal activities while almost 225,000 of their fellow citizens, just 1,200 hundred miles to the north, had died or were missing, and hundreds of thousands more were left homeless and suffering.

I'm happy to say my perception was wrong. I even feel a little embarrassed now to have had the thought, because our flight, a wide-body DC-10 carrying over 300 hundred passengers, was full of Indonesian doctors, nurses, teachers, and students heading to Banda Aceh to help their fellow citizens.

Chapter Eleven

Ground Zero

Banda Aceh, Indonesia

Our plane landed in Banda Aceh at noon on February 2. The approach to the airport allowed us a glimpse of the tsunami devastated coastline. Seeing the devastation on television did not compare to what we saw from the plane's windows. Water still filled much of the low-lying inland areas. The coastal areas were dark brown in color, devoid of vegetation and structures—an extreme contrast to the other coastal areas of Sumatra that were green and lush with vegetation.

Stepping onto the tarmac, we were unprepared for the extreme heat and humidity. It was hotter than Jakarta and compared favorably to being inside of a steam bath. The airport was very small. So small, in fact, that we disembarked on the tarmac and then walked to the airport building, a huge contrast to Jakarta's modern airport. The chaotic baggage claim area was a room no larger than twenty feet by fifty feet with no air conditioning. The small conveyer belt for luggage was surrounded by a mix of people of different cultures and languages, shoving and pushing at each other to claim their baggage.

As we waited for our backpacks and materials, all of a sudden Samuel Soh, an Indonesian Christian working for World Harvest, appeared. He recognized us immediately because of our World Harvest shirts and hats.

The short stocky Indonesian man with Chinese features spoke English with an Asian accent. He proved he was a "can-do" person right away as he secured a porter and cart to get our large packages and whisked us out into the airport parking lot. The parking lot was a jumble of confusion like the baggage hall. Cars, trucks, motorcycles, and even people jostled for the limited space in front of the airport arrival hall. Hundreds of vehicles bore identification placards of various organizations and countries, all waiting to receive their new arrivals. The truck that would transport us and our electrical supplies was right outside the building, commanding a prominent place among the hundreds of other vehicles.

The airport was several miles inland from the major damage along the coast, and had suffered only minor damage, closing for just one day after the earthquake and tsunami. Crammed with our bags and materials into the back of an enclosed truck without air conditioning, we set off for the house used by World Harvest as its base camp. We sat on bench seats arranged along the sides of the truck. Luckily there were windows to open in the back and the driver drove as fast as he could to keep the air flowing.

Although we'd seen so much devastation on the tip of Sumatra from the airplane windows, we didn't see any damage on the ground until we got closer to base camp, which was five miles from the airport. Even then, the major destruction occurred along the beach areas and in downtown Banda Aceh.

The three-bedroom house stood on the outskirts of Banda Aceh, in an area that had escaped the horrific effects of the tsunami. The house was being rented by World Harvest from a local Muslim family, who had moved in with nearby relatives. The owner's wife, Anda, who had been hired by World Harvest to act as treasurer for their ongoing projects in the Aceh province, worked at the base camp house during the day.

The green tin roof home with gray outer walls was built of cinderblock and concrete. In front was a small covered porch with a table and chairs; an attached garage had been converted to a medical center. Well cared for flowers and bushes surrounded the home. There was no air conditioning but the house did have about a dozen fans. The fans kept the air moving and disrupted the pesky biting flies that came inside freely as the windows had no screens. Once inside, and because I'd taken DEET as insect repellant, the mosquitoes didn't bother me. But that didn't hold true when we visited the refugee camp at night. Those mosquitoes were unfazed by the DEET and ate me alive!

After we had dumped our materials in the garage, we received our first introduction to an Indonesian custom—the removal of shoes before entering a residence, which we later learned also included a tent. When I walked into the house with shoes on, one of Indonesian interpreters saw me and quickly said, "Oh no, you have to take your shoes off." I had seen a pile of shoes outside on the porch but hadn't taken the hint.

Once inside, we were offered lunch consisting of spicy rice and a small piece of fried chicken wrapped in a palm leaf, our first home-cooked meal in Indonesia.

After lunch, Samuel announced he was ready to take us on a tour of the decimated areas and on the way back we'd stop at the camp. "In Indonesia," Samuel explained, "they don't refer to the camps using the term refugee; instead they are referred to as an Internal Displaced Persons Camp, or IDP Camp, for short."

* * * * *

Before leaving base camp, Samuel handed each of us a paper-thin blue dust mask. "These are just a precaution," he said. "Sometimes we drive through areas where the air still reeks of dead bodies."

Once again we crammed into the back of the enclosed truck that had brought us from the airport. Samuel sat up front with the driver and directed him to head west on the main road out of Banda Aceh toward the Lhok Nga district.

We sat on the narrow bench seats in the rear passenger compartment with a Korean pastor and two associates who had come to Banda Aceh on a scouting mission to see how their church might contribute to the ongoing relief operations. An Indonesian gentleman, Pastor Himawan Hadirahardja, also came along. We later learned that he was the World Harvest Director for Focus on the Family Indonesia.

We'd driven less than a mile when the first evidence of tsunami destruction appeared. Partially damaged houses, crushed vehicles, and uprooted trees dotted the sodden landscape along the unmarked narrow two-lane asphalt road.

But the scene changed rapidly as we drove deeper into the decimated area. Grayish-brown mud and debris partially covered the road, making it difficult to navigate. Occasionally, we dodged an orange or black body bag placed along the road to await collection for burial. Samuel told us how beautiful the area had once been with lush greenery, nice homes, a golf course and attractive shops. Still, with so much destruction, it was hard for us to picture how things must have been.

On one narrow curve in the road I spotted a small clock sitting upright in the broken branches of a small tree. Its hands were frozen on 8:46, the exact time the waves had completed their destructive assault and began their retreat to the sea. Someone had found it in the debris and placed it in the tree as a memorial to the people who had perished and as a reminder to those who had survived. It was a solemn moment for all of us. On another trip to the camp, we stopped and I took a photo of the clock.

Closer to Lhok Nga, cluttered debris fields as far as the eye could see replaced the earlier damage. Miles and miles of debris that had once been prosperous and thriving communities now resembled a wasteland.

Even today, it is difficult to describe how we felt when we discovered that the beach communities of the Lhok Nga district had completely washed away. Feelings of sadness, grief, and heartfelt sorrow caused some of us to cry and others to grieve silently, as we struggled privately to understand what had happened there.

The only semblance of humanity that remained was the Mosque at Lampuuk, which had survived almost intact, but the more than 1,500 people who had sought protection there had perished. As we surveyed the damage, we saw small fragments from the walls of homes lying haphazardly against the few remaining trees that had somehow miraculously survived the onslaught. We also saw the remains of cement slabs, which had served as foundations for the thousands of homes that had made up the beach communities of Lhok Nga.

Further down the beach, we saw a large fully loaded coal barge and its tugboat escort that had been deposited on shore. It was an eerie scene—both sat upright on the beach about 300 yards inland and seemed to be quietly waiting for the wave to come back and return them to the ocean to continue their disrupted voyage.

Leaving the beach area, we passed an open mass grave that held several hundred bodies, each enclosed in a body bag. "They don't suffer anymore," Samuel explained, speaking from the front seat through a small window that opened into the rear compartment of the truck. "Now we'll visit the camp and you'll meet the ones suffering, the ones who God sent you here to help."

His words put everything in perspective. God had a plan to help a suffering people—the people of IDP Camp #85. He revealed part of His plan to me on the fifth of January and formed our small group. He'd provided all the resources we needed, the specific contacts we needed, and sent us to this particular camp where we'd be His hands, His arms, His love, and His comfort.

* * * * *

IDP Camp #85 (or *Posko 85* in Indonesian), sits off the main road from Lhok Nga in a grove of coconut and palm trees. It was a small oasis in an area that had been completely destroyed by the tsunami. The camp of 250 tents, which is about ten miles from base camp and four miles inland from the beach, is almost equally divided by a narrow, pot-holed, single-lane dirt road. It had no running water and no electricity for lights.

Samuel escorted us throughout the camp and told us that our work would begin the following day. We finally laid eyes on the mystery generator. It was the first opportunity for Pastor Eric and Richard to get acquainted with the generator—a 13kVA Atlas Copco (QAS 14). The generator was a skid-based mobile generator with a maximum current of 20 amps. Pastor Eric wrote down the manufacturer's information and made a note to call the master electrician back home for instructions on making the necessary connections.

* * * * *

Back at base camp for dinner, we were introduced to several other relief workers living in the house: a four-person emergency medical team from Australia, an Indonesian doctor and nurse team, and several Indonesian counselors and translators. The crowded house would be our home for the next few days.

Samuel explained that the women occupied two of the bedrooms and the Australian medical team had the third bedroom. He and the other Indonesian men, and the group from Korea, slept on mats in the large living room area, so we'd have to bed down in the small front entry hall. Thin mats had already been arranged for us on the tile floor.

After dropping our backpacks, we were shown to a bathroom to wash for dinner. The small enclosed space, no larger than a closet, consisted of a waist-high concrete basin with a faucet, which supplied only cold water. The basin remained filled with brown murky water for bathing and doubled as a water reservoir for a Western-style toilet that lacked a tank or flushing mechanism. Thankfully, we had remembered to bring our own toilet paper.

The Indonesian relief workers were preparing the dinner meal in a small primitive kitchen, adjacent to the bathroom, which had a sink, a stove hooked to a propane tank, and a tiny old-fashioned refrigerator. Its freezer, probably never defrosted, was so iced over it was unusable.

We learned quickly that their meals always consisted of spicy rice or noodles with beef or chicken wrapped in palm leaves. On occasion the chefs substituted an unidentifiable meat for the chicken and beef. The Australians called it mystery meat. What a contrast to our brief stay in the posh Jakarta hotel!

We sat in the large living room area talking with the other relief workers while waiting for dinner. The room was sparsely furnished with a large leather sofa. Those who couldn't fit on the sofa sat on the tile floor on their bedrolls. There were two low cabinets in the room, which were used as a television stand and a desk for several laptop computers. The television only provided a limited choice of three Indonesian-language stations. The laptops were hardly used because the Internet connection seldom worked. After dinner, when all the volunteers were assembled at base camp, Samuel would ask what had happened during the day in order to prepare his daily report.

On our first night, while we were waiting for dinner, Pastor Eric spotted what looked like an IV connection on the hand of one of the Australian women. He asked her directly, "Is that an IV?"

"It sure is. I got salmonella poisoning from eating the food," she replied, then warned, "You really have to be careful."

"In this house?" Pastor Eric asked, the alarm audible in his voice as he remembered we had heartily consumed the lunch that was offered when we arrived.

"Yes, here!" came the blunt reply. Moments later, she was up and running for the bathroom where faint sounds of vomiting could be heard.

We exchanged concerned glances. Without speaking, it was understood that we'd have to pass on dinner, even if it meant disrespecting our hosts. I found an unopened can of baked beans, Richard fixed spaghetti, one of the military ready-to-eat meals, and Pastor Eric feasted on a bag of spicy, semi-soft candies he'd brought from the States. Apparently unfazed by the warning, Roy Ramalingam continued to enjoy the local food. Praise be to God, he never got sick.

Chapter Twelve

First Day, First Light

The next morning we were up early, eager to get started. We had set a goal to have at least one light working by the end of our first day.

As I headed to the primitive bathroom to brush my teeth with the bottled water I had been provided, I passed through the kitchen and noticed the Indonesians preparing a breakfast of fried eggs with noodles and toast. I must admit that the smells coming from the kitchen were delicious. With a watering mouth, I reluctantly declined the hot breakfast in favor of my own instant oatmeal and coffee, which I prepared with bottled water.

After breakfast we loaded up the truck with our equipment and materials and headed out to the camp to begin our work. It was still early morning when we left.

At the camp, we divided into two teams, Pastor Eric and Richard concentrated on the generator while Roy and I, along with several young Indonesian volunteers, began stringing the cable in the trees along the narrow dirt road and in the trees along the path to the makeshift toilets and showers.

By mid-morning, the generator team had made good progress wiring the generator to the panel box. Before powering up the generator, however, Pastor Eric wanted to check with the master electrician back in the States. It was a good time to call, too, because there was a twelve-hour time difference between Maryland and our location.

In order to get sufficient signal strength to use Lew's worldwide phone, Pastor Eric had to climb one of the nearby hills. He took along one of the Indonesian translators, just in case he met up with a rebel patrol or somehow got lost.

He returned shortly and told us he wasn't successful finding a place with enough signal strength to make the call, so we just had to do the best we could. We were still hopeful that some parts of the camp would have lights by evening.

Sometime later, Richard came to tell us that the Chief of the camp, wanting to show his appreciation for our efforts, had invited him into his tent for fried bananas and pre-packaged, partially gelled Jell-O we would have to suck through a straw. He invited us to return with him to the Chief's tent.

It was a wonderful break. We found the fried bananas very tasty. We only considered eating the bananas because they were deep-fried. From that time on, we looked forward to our banana treat every day we were in the camp.

Lunch arrived at the camp a few hours later—more of the spicy rice from the night before, but this time, the chicken had been replaced with the mystery meat the Australians had warned us about. I put my portion aside. Richard had filled up on a double portion of fried bananas and Pastor Eric continued to feast from his bottomless bag of candy he'd brought from home. Roy remained unfazed and enjoyed his Indonesian lunch.

Our afternoon work consisted of connecting the light fixtures to the cable. Richard used one of the pigtails he and Pastor Eric had constructed at the hotel in Jakarta to make our first light connection. Pastor Eric turned on the generator and flipped the breaker switch. With baited breath we waited and then, when we saw that the light worked, we began to celebrate, each man thanking God for His abundant favor.

We quickly moved to connect additional light fixtures to the cable. Richard demonstrated how to make the pigtail connection to several of the local Indonesian men who had helped string the cable. They were fast learners. With their help, our work progressed quickly. Roy then organized his own work team of Indonesians and strung cable and lights from the road to the makeshift toilets and showers at the edge of the camp.

By late afternoon, lights had been placed every fifteen to twenty feet along both sides of the road and along the path to the toilets and bath stalls. Pastor Eric decided to test each run of lights separately. He started with the lights that ran along the road, but an unexpected electrical overload tripped the breaker.

We scrambled to find the reason for the overload. Richard walked the length of the cable all the way to the main road. There he noticed that a local merchant, who sold tea, soft drinks, biscuits, and clove cigarettes from a crudely built lean-to, which he had named "The Tsunami Cafe," had tied into one of our pigtails, causing the overload. Fortunately for him, he had done the deed before the electricity had been turned on; otherwise he would have been electrocuted. Pastor Eric inspected the splice and with a snip of his cable cutters the problem was quickly resolved and the lights restored.

Just as soon as we'd solved that problem another popped up. A French group, Pompiers *Sans Frontieres* (Firemen without Borders), had set up their base camp at the front and along one side of the narrow dirt road that led into IDP Camp #85. There were about twenty of them, all dressed in firemen's gear: white T-shirts, grey pants with pale yellow suspenders and boots. They had rigged up a giant parachute-like cover over picnic tables and folding chairs to shield them from the sun. Being very territorial, they objected to the cable being hung on the side of the road that bordered their camp. We raised the cable higher and higher, but they continued to protest our cable was too low and would prevent their re-supply trucks from entering their camp.

During our exchange with the French firemen, Richard noticed they had a refrigeration unit and that some of the firemen were drinking cold sodas while others had glasses of water with ice. He approached the French firemen with Lusiana "Lusi" Rumintang, our Indonesian translator, who also spoke French. The only thing cold they received was the cold shoulder treatment when they asked the firemen to share some of their veritable treasure with us or allow us to buy some from them.

While we were dealing with the French, Pastor Eric wired the mosque for lights and connected its loud speaker to the electrical loop. This was very important because the *Muezzin*, (a man appointed to call the people for prayer) uses a loudspeaker to hasten Muslims to the mosque five times a day: at dawn, midday, the middle of the afternoon, just after sunset, and finally about two hours after sunset.

It was getting late in the day when we finally concluded that no matter how high we placed the cable, there was no way to please the French firemen. We decided to remove all of the cable that bordered the French base camp, then packed up so we could return to base camp for dinner and a good night's rest.

When we headed back to base camp between 5 and 6:00 p.m., we saw numerous bodies in body bags along the road, waiting to be picked up by the military. Too much time had passed for identifying bodies; they were bloated and decomposing rapidly, so these bodies would be placed in huge mass graves.

* * * * *

When we got back to base camp, the house had become a little more comfortable. The Korean pastor and his associates and the Australian team had departed for home, leaving us alone in the house with Samuel and the remaining Indonesian relief workers. Richard, the master plumber, and I moved into the bedroom vacated by the Australians, to give more space to Eric, the Assistant Pastor, and Roy, the fitness center manager, in the small entry hall.

Dinner that night consisted of fried noodles and beef (at least I think it was beef). It smelled good as it usually did. Deciding once again not to risk getting sick, Richard and I declined politely. We'd share the peanut butter crackers he'd brought from home, and of course, Pastor Eric continued to feast on candy. Our decision left more food for the others to enjoy. Ironically, despite all my precautions, I came home with intestinal problems that lasted two weeks. Needless to say I spent a lot of time in the bathroom.

After dinner, we had the driver take us back to the camp so we could check the lighting. Pastor Hadirahardja and Lusi accompanied us. They'd helped us throughout the day and had become honorary members of our team. Both would leave for Jakarta two days later. Pastor Hadirahardja would be replaced by Pastor Jacob, the pastor at World Harvest headquarters who had given us the backpacks. Lusi would be replaced by Risma Saragih, an Indonesian working in America who had left her home in Florida to return to Indonesia to help out in Banda Aceh.

Except for the dim headlights of the truck, we drove to the camp in pitch-black darkness. Occasionally we saw a campfire in the distance but there were no lights to be seen until we arrived at the camp. Everything was working well and the people of the camp showed their appreciation for the lights with smiles and handshakes.

Children scampered about playing with their crude toys, even if they were no more than simple sticks. They seem to have adjusted well despite their hardships; they were very friendly and smiled all the time. While we had worked on the lights, many of them followed us around and watched. Several humanitarian organizations provided teachers for the camp, giving the children a chance to attend school for at least a few hours a day.

Just before heading back to our base camp, we heard the crackle of the loud speaker and the voice of the *Muezzin* calling the people to prayer. It was truly a time of rejoicing.

Chapter Thirteen

A Time of Bonding

Upon our return to base camp, Samuel assembled everyone in the living room for the nightly debriefing. These meetings provided an opportunity for all of us to share how we'd spent our day and to give Samuel information for his daily report to World Harvest. Samuel and the other Indonesians congratulated us on our progress and applauded our work ethic.

After the briefing, Richard suggested we get together in our bedroom for devotion. He invited the other Indonesian houseguests to join us. We sat in a tight circle praying and taking turns sharing our Christian experiences and our reasons for coming to Banda Aceh. The four of us told about our church, which had been active in mission work for the past couple of years. Indonesia was the furthest any of us had gone to help out. In addition to being a time of reflection and a time to seek God, it was also a time of bonding with our Indonesian hosts.

Samuel was asked about his reasons for coming to Banda Aceh. We were all touched by his incredible story, which I shared in the beginning of this book.

As I listened to his story, I remembered Jeremiah 1:5 and realized that God had already put His plan in place before anyone knew the tsunami would hit: before the people on that hill began to cry out and pray for God's help, and before the people of IDP Camp #85 knew they would need lights.

I know now His plan didn't start with me and it won't end with me, but I'm so grateful to have been a part of it.

Chapter Fourteen

Lighting the Darkness

Instilled with fresh enthusiasm, the next morning we began running new lengths of cable into the interior of the camp. Around 10:00 a.m., we assembled near the chief's tent, hoping for another invitation to feast on the delicious fried bananas. We were not disappointed.

At lunchtime, our driver arrived with instructions to bring us back to base camp for a hot lunch. We decided to remain at the camp to continue the wiring. By late afternoon, Pastor Eric had wired the water pumps to the panel box, giving the people a steady supply of water for showers, cooking, and cleaning.

That evening at base camp, Pastor Eric and Richard wanted to celebrate our progress with dinner in a restaurant. They asked Samuel if there were any local restaurants open for dinner. Samuel didn't know of any, but Pastor Himawan knew of one that had recently reopened on the road to the airport. He agreed to take us there.

I knew my fellow team members were hoping for a hamburger or maybe even a steak. I was hoping for some real food, too, because we'd gone two days without eating a full meal. Roy was the only one eating because he really enjoyed the Indonesian food.

Imagine our disappointment when the driver pulled up in front of a dingy roadside restaurant that only served more of the spicy rice and noodle dishes, which Pastor Himawan ordered for everyone. Having seen how the cooking was done so near the roadway that the dust from passing cars couldn't help but blow into the food, I decided against eating it.

When we arrived back at base camp and assembled for our nightly debriefing, Pastor Eric told Samuel and the group that the remaining work would be completed ahead of schedule—in three and a half days instead of six or seven days. Samuel could hardly believe it. He wanted to visit the camp that night to see the results of the work so far.

At the camp, Samuel was amazed at how much work we'd already accomplished. Lights hung from the trees illuminating almost all of the camp. People were gathered together talking and laughing under the lights. The camp's Chief talked with Samuel and thanked him for improving life at the camp.

Samuel became emotional as he grappled to find the right words to thank us for what we had done. He told us how the camp's residents had watched each day as relief workers from various organizations walked through the camp and asked questions to complete their surveys. The organizations had promised relief—but nothing was ever done, and the Chief and the people had been disappointed so many times. Aid efforts had concentrated on water, medicine, food and shelter for the Indonesian survivors, but the other things like lights, refrigeration, and employment had been overlooked. Since the arrival of the doctors, he told us, our lighting project was the first time someone had done something to improve the well-being of his people.

On the drive back to base camp, Samuel, a strong man of God and proud of his Indonesian heritage, continued to thank us and tell us how important the lights were to him and the people in the camp.

* * * * *

The next morning was Friday, the Muslim holy day. All work would have to stop just before the start of the afternoon prayer. We only had two strings of lights remaining to be hung and we were determined to complete the lighting project before then.

Soon after starting, we were interrupted by a delegation from the French firemen's camp. The delegation now wanted to negotiate for some of our electrical materials because they wanted to duplicate our lighting efforts around their camp. In exchange for providing the materials, the French promised to supply us with cold drinks and ice.

Looking forward to cooling refreshments, we agreed and gave the French delegation twice the amount of material they had requested and even showed them how to make the pigtail connection between the light fixture and the cable. When the French returned, they brought us only two cold cans of Coke and two cold liter bottles of water. We felt shanghaied--it didn't seem like a fair exchange.

We didn't spend much time worrying about our trade, as we still had more work to do. The Indonesians had seen the unfair exchange. Shortly afterward, one of the older Indonesian men, using only a circle of cloth around his feet, shimmied up a nearby seventy-foot coconut tree and cut down about ten green coconuts, which the others retrieved. They cut them open for us, and to our surprise, the coconut juice inside was more satisfying than the cold drinks and water. More than that, it was a unifying moment for the American Christians and the Indonesian Muslims in the camp.

After a short break for our daily ration of fried bananas with the Chief, we finished wiring the remaining areas of the camp. We had gotten it done before afternoon prayers! Before returning to base camp to report our success, we were joined by the Chief's son and many of the camp's residents. They came to thank us and tell us how much the lights meant to them.

Many in the camp were very superstitious and believed the dead were walking around. Several residents had made special requests to put a light closer to their tent. We placed as many as we could. We'd brought lights enough for each tent, but we soon discovered the panel box restricted the number we used to approximately one hundred. We left what remained of the supplies with the young men we'd trained to replace the bulbs and to make additional pigtail connections, if needed.

I'd brought a duffel bag full of gifts to give away on the last day. We gave out toy cars, jump ropes, soccer balls, a baseball glove and other things, as well as clothes and candy. To the Chief's son, we gave money for the men who had helped us install the lights. We took lots of group photos with our new family.

On our way back to base camp, Risma Saragih, our Indonesian translator (who had been living and working in the United States before the tsunami struck), asked our driver to stop at the outdoor marketplace so she could buy a durian. Roy had heard about this very foul-smelling, green almond-shaped fruit with spikes, but the rest of us hadn't. Named the King of fruits, it was considered a Southeast Asian delicacy. Risma called it a "stinky fruit." Richard decided to try it and liked it, but the smell repulsed me and the others.

Later that night we returned to the camp to make sure that the lights were working properly and to say our final goodbyes to our new brothers and sisters.

* * * * *

The next morning, Samuel surprised us by announcing that we would be leaving that very morning on the 11:30 a.m. flight to Jakarta. With little more than two hours before the flight, we rushed to pack our gear. Before going to the airport we needed to make another stop at IDP Camp #85 because Samuel needed to take more photos of the camp to send to World Harvest.

Chapter Fifteen

Reflections

On the flight to Jakarta, I sat in a window seat, staring out at the giant columns of cumulus cloud formations in the distance. Somehow being up there made me feel closer to God. I began to reflect on all that we had accomplished, hoping that our work in the camp was pleasing and acceptable to God.

Thinking back on our trip, I recalled Pastor Eric's words from one of our early devotion sessions in Jakarta before we departed for Banda Aceh: "Just as Jesus brought light to the world, God, in his infinite wisdom and mercy, is allowing us to bring a symbolic light to the people in the camp." His enlightened words had made us realize just how special our assignment had been and how important it was for us to have come.

I recalled the fifth of January when God had placed the burden on my heart and an urging in my spirit to go to Banda Aceh—a Muslim stronghold on the other side of the world.

Immediately, the devil came in and tried to discourage me. He wanted me to believe it was just a crazy, harebrained idea. He offered a zillion excuses for not going. By the mercy of God, my teammates and I chose to believe

God and leave our homes, our families, and our jobs to travel halfway around the world to a place we'd never visited, to help a people that we did not even know.

Today, we are better men, better Christians because we listened to God and trusted Him. It wasn't easy in the beginning because I tried to take control of everything, but as I yielded to God, things fell into place and our trip became a wonderful adventure and a great learning experience.

God has personally taught me so much through this experience, especially about the plans and purposes that He has for each of us. To help me understand His plan for my life, He showed me that His overall plan for mankind is made up of individual plans that are unique to each person. They are spiritual connections, inestimable in number and of differing lengths, reaching out in the spiritual world waiting to be released through our lives into the physical world.

At certain times and places our paths will cross someone else's path. For a mere moment, God's plans for both our lives are joined until they separate again. These are divine appointments setup by God for us to bless or be blessed by others. Such was the case for our team when God crossed our paths with the paths of Samuel Soh and the people of IDP Camp #85 in Banda Aceh, Indonesia.

As I sat peering out of the giant aircraft's window, I recalled another appointment that had occurred at 8:30 p.m. on November 23, 2003, when I crossed paths with a visiting pastor, Basil Yarde, who was speaking at my church. He asked the congregation to remove their socks and shoes and come to the front of the sanctuary so he could bless our feet. I went to the front and when it was my turn he knelt in front of me, placed his hands on my feet and prayed. His exact words were, "I anoint your feet to take hope to the hopeless." Remembering his words reminded me of just how awesome God is.

God has preordained divine appointments for all of us. All we have to do is make ourselves available for God to use us. And when we do, God will be faithful and move heaven and earth to accomplish His plan in our lives.

Epilogue

Several large aftershocks from the devastating December 26, 2004, earthquake have since jolted the city of Banda Aceh. Another giant earthquake, measuring 8.7 on the Richter scale struck at 11:09 p.m. on March 29, 2005. It also produced several large aftershocks. Each of the quakes caused mass panic all over the city. Terrified and confused, people remembered the tsunami that came ashore after the first earthquake and ran for higher ground. Many screamed as they ran, "Water is coming! Water is coming from the west coast area...run, run!" Each time, Samuel and others attempted to calm everyone.

As tsunami survivors in the Indian Ocean region continue to struggle to reclaim their lives, Christian volunteers, like Samuel Soh and others working with IES and World Harvest, are still there, demonstrating the love of Christ through their work.

They need our prayers and they need our continued financial support. I'm donating all proceeds from this book to the people of IDP Camp #85, to help them recover from the disastrous tsunami. You can help, too, by sending a tax-deductible contribution to:

World Harvest
c/o IDP Camp #85
P.O. Box 187
Monterey Park, CA 91754-0187

Afterword

Did God Cause The Tsunami?

While I'm not a theologian, I feel compelled to address this question. Some Christian and Muslim leaders have stated publicly that God caused the tsunami because of the sin of the people in that area. I strongly, but respectfully, disagree. I do, however, agree with one premise of their statement—that God, who is sovereign and ultimately in control of all things, allowed the tsunami to occur. The difference between allowing something to occur and causing something to occur may seem minuscule, but I think, is important to consider.

Using the Bible as reference, I begin in the book of Genesis, Chapter 1, where God created the heavens and the earth, and every living thing. He gave man a free will and complete dominion over all the earth. In Chapter 3, Adam and Eve yield to Satan's deception and thereby conveyed their dominion of God's creation to Satan. God confronted the man and the woman and announced in verse 17 that because of this sin, "...*cursed is the ground because of you,*" and they were forced out of the Garden of Eden.

God was in control of the Garden of Eden just as He is in control over all things today, but He did not stop Satan from entering or from confronting Adam and Eve or stop them from committing sin. Although God allowed sin to happen, He did not cause it. And through the disobedience of

87

Adam and Eve, the Bible says that all mankind became spiritually separated from God (or spiritually dead) and sin and death entered into the world. (Romans 5:12).

God had made a perfect world and gave dominion of that perfect world to man, who in turn negligently transferred that dominion and authority to Satan. Outside of the Garden of Eden the land was cursed by God. It is still cursed today. Romans Chapter 8, verse 22 says, *"We know that the whole creation has been groaning as in the pains of childbirth right up to the present time* [waiting for the return of Jesus, who will defeat Satan and restore dominion to God]."

Satan is now the ruler of this world (II Corinthians 4:4) and the prince of the air (Ephesians 2:2), and his dominion includes principalities and powers, rulers of the darkness of this world, and spiritual forces of wickedness in high places (Ephesians 6:12). Satan's nature, and his very purpose is to kill, steal, and destroy. (John 10:10). He is mankind's adversary, who, like a roaring lion, walks around seeking those he may devour. (I Peter 5:8).

When Satan confronted Jesus in the wilderness (Matthew 4:8-9), he took Jesus to a very high mountain and showed Him all the kingdoms of the world (and all their glory). Satan told Jesus that he would give him all of those things if Jesus would simply fall down and worship him. If Satan didn't have control of the kingdoms of this world, the temptation of Jesus would have been invalid.

It's a fact that in the Old Testament, God pronounced many judgments on the people because of their sin—their perverse nature. Each time, God either told righteous men of His impending judgment (e.g., Noah and Abraham) or sent messengers to warn the people to repent (e.g., the Old Testament prophets) or in the case of the destruction of Sodom and Gomorrah, he sent Angels to bring out the righteous to safety.

In the New Testament, Jesus did not come to judge the world: *"For God did not send his Son into the world to condemn the world, but to save the world through him."* (John 3:17).

Jesus came to restore mankind's relationship to God. The Bible is replete with references to the reconciliation of mankind to God by Jesus Christ. For example, II Corinthians, Chapter 5, verses 17-19 says, *"Therefore, if anyone is in Christ, he is a new creation; the old has gone, the new has come! All this is from God, who reconciled us to himself through Christ and gave us the ministry of reconciliation: that God was reconciling the world to himself in Christ, not counting men's sins against them. And he has committed to us the message of reconciliation."*

This reconciliation is ongoing. The only judgment God has pronounced on mankind since the coming of His Son, Jesus Christ, is found in John 3:18-19, which reads, *"Whoever believes in him [Jesus] is not condemned, but whoever does not believe stands condemned already because he has not believed in the name of God's one and only Son. This is the verdict: Light has come into the world, but men loved darkness instead of light because their deeds were evil."*

The Bible says to be very careful not to pass judgment on people who have suffered misfortune. It is for God alone to judge. There is a story in the Bible where Jesus warns the people not to be harsh in judging the misfortune of others: *"Now there were some present at that time who told Jesus about the Galileans whose blood Pilate had mixed with their sacrifices. Jesus answered, Do you think that these Galileans were worse sinners than all the other Galileans because they suffered this way?"* **[In other words, do you think the people who perished in the tsunami were worse sinners than all of us because they perished that way?]** Jesus answers the question in verse 3, *"I tell you, no! But unless you repent, you too will all perish. Or those eighteen who died when the tower in Siloam fell on them - do you think they were more guilty than all the others living in Jerusalem? I tell you, no! But unless you repent, you too will all perish."* (Luke 13:1-5).

A terrible tragedy occurred on December 26, 2004, as a result of an undersea earthquake that generated a massive tsunami. It was not, in my humble opinion, caused by the hand of God. Many lives were lost and many lives were ruined. The estimates of the number of dead and missing range from 250,000 to 288,000 and, because of the enormity of the destruction, the real number may never be known.

Rather than pronounce judgment on those who have suffered, let us pray for their salvation—for their reconciliation with God.

Acknowledgments

I wish to express my sincere appreciation to my fellow team members: Pastor Eric Dorsey, Roy Ramalingam, and Richard Bell, and to our pastor, St. Clair Mitchell of Evangel Assembly of God Church, Camp Springs, Maryland, for believing in the vision God gave me for the people of Banda Aceh, and for stepping out in faith to help the people of the Internal Displaced Persons Camp #85.

As a team we owe a deep debt of gratitude to our wives and children, who fully supported our journey to Indonesia, and to our relatives, friends, neighbors, and co-workers, and our church family for supporting us with their generous financial contributions, along with their prayers.

Along the way we met some wonderful people who helped make our journey memorable. Our special thanks to David and Kelley, a husband and wife flight attendant team we met in the rear coach section on Northwest Flight 11. They made the long flight to Tokyo enjoyable. Thanks to the extended family of Roy Ramalingam, who met us at the airport in Singapore in the early morning hours during our seven-hour layover, and to Robert, a fellow passenger on our flight from Singapore to Jakarta, who provided some well-needed advice about getting around in Indonesia.

On the ground in Indonesia, we were blessed by Dave Kenney, Pastor of the International English Service Church in Jakarta, who hosted our visit. He treated us like royalty and introduced us to Lew Belcourt of World Harvest, a great missionary and blessed man of God, who provided us the opportunity to help the residents of IDP Camp #85. We were especially blessed by the 1,500 residents of IDP Camp #85. Although devout Muslims, they opened the camp and their temporary homes to us and welcomed us as friends and brothers.

Thanks also to my editors, Victoria Giraud and Allan Manuel, best of all editors, who worked exceptionally hard and long to help me give voice to a wonderful, Spirit-filled story.

Lastly, but most importantly—none of this would have been possible without the vision, favor, and presence of the Lord Jesus Christ, who met our every need.